GLOBAL TOURISM POLICIES, LAWS & ACTION PLANS

GLOBAL TOURISM POLICIES, LAWS & ACTION PLANS
Select Case Studies and Model Approaches

Edited by
Dr. P.C. Sinha

SBS Publishers & Distributors Pvt. Ltd.
New Delhi

ISBN : 81-89741-29-2

Global Tourism Policies, Laws, Action Plans: Select Case Studies and Model Approaches

First Published in India in 2006

© Dr. P.C. Sinha

Published by:
SBS PUBLISHERS & DISTRIBUTORS PVT. LTD.
2/9, Ground Floor, Ansari Road, Darya Ganj,
New Delhi - 110002, INDIA.
Tel: 0091-11-23289119 / 41563911
Email: mail@sbspublishers.com

Printed at
Chaman Enterprises
1603, Pataudi House,Daryaganj
New Delhi 110002

Preface

This book titled "Global Tourism Policies, Laws, Action Plans: Select Case Studies and Model Approaches" gives readers an overview of ongoing developments in this area of study. Select case studies and model approaches have been presented to elaborate upon the global tourism policies, laws and action plans.

The first chapter of this book deals with contemporary trends in global tourism, including the sustainable tourism. A WTO perspective on the whole issue is provided, detailing very issues involved. An indepth analysis of sustainable tourism policies and action plan is provided for reader's perusal. the second chapter deals with model tourism policies. Case studies of Guyana, India and Andhra Pradesh are provided so that a balanced picture on the said issue could emerge.

The third chapter deals with a model law regulating the activities of travel agencies, tour guides and transferists. A Case Study of Macau is presented to elaborate upon the issue.

The fourth chapter concerns with model laws, policies and action plans concerning sex-tourism of children world wide. The US policy in this regard is presented the international cooperation required for curbing sex-tourism of children globally is dealt briefly, including the human rights perspective.

The detailed analysis of World Congress against commercial sexual exploitation of children is presented. Other policies and action plans in this regard mainly those of important international organizations are presented.

The last chapter deals with various action plans for tourism from all over the world, such as that of the Commonwealth, Anglesey, Wellington and Canada.

In sum, this book could work as an eye-opener for those who are trying to understand global tourism laws, policies, action plans and strategies. The book is user-friendly and provides both third-world and developed countries perspective on the subject.

Dr. P.C. Sinha

Contents

Glossary

ABTA: Association of British Travel Agents. The trade association of large tour operators.

Aboriginal: Refers to the original inhabitants of a country and their descendants. The term is used mainly in Australia and Canada.

All-inclusive: A resort providing accommodation, food and all facilities (e.g. beach and watersports) internally, so that visitors have no need to leave the resort.

ATOL: Air Travel Organizers Licence. A bonding scheme run by the Civil Aviation Authority. If your tour operator is a member of ATOL, you are guaranteed a refund if the company goes into liquidation.

Backpacker: A (usually young) independent traveller; typically carries a rucksack and stays in cheap, locally owned accommodation.

Canopy walkway: A constructed bridge walkway through the tree tops of a forest.

Community: A mutually supportive, geographically specific social unit such as a rural village or tribe. In an urban, Western context, the phrase is often used more loosely, to describe people with common interests, ethnic origins, etc.

Community-based tourism: Tourism that consults, involves and benefits a local community, especially in the context of rural villages in developing countries and indigenous peoples.

Conservation (nature): Protection against irreversible destruction and other undesirable changes, including the management of human use of organisms or ecosystems to ensure such use is sustainable.

Conservation enterprises: Income generating activities that focus on conserving natural resources and ecosystems.

Customised itineraries: A holiday schedule drawn up by a tour operator specifically for one client or group, usually including flight, accommodation and transport. Sometimes called tailor-made holidays.

Developing countries/nations/world: The world's less wealthy nations, mostly former colonies: i.e. most of Asia, Africa, Latin America and the South Pacific. Also sometimes referred to as *the South*.

Development: A process of economic and social transformation that defies simple definition. Though often viewed as a strictly economic process involving growth and diversification of a country's economy, development is a qualitative concept that entails complex social, cultural, and environmental changes. There are many models of what 'development' should look like and many different standards of what constitutes 'success'.

Domestic tourism: Holidays taken within the tourist's own country. The volume of domestic tourism is hard to quantify but has been estimated at three to five times greater than international tourism.

Ecology: Originally defined by Ernst Haeckel in 1866, ecology is the study of the relationships that develop among living organisms and between these organisms and the environment.

Economic growth: The change over a period of time in the value (monetary and non-monetary) of goods and services and the ability and capacity to produce goods and services. It is economic growth which generates the wealth necessary to provide social services, health care, and education. It is the basis for ongoing job creation. However, sustainable development requires that there be a change in the nature of economic growth, to ensure that goods and services are produced by environmentally sound and economically sustainable processes. This will require efficient use of resources, value-added processing, sustained yield management of renewable resources, and the consideration and accounting of all externalities and side-effects involved in the extraction, processing, production, distribution, consumption, and disposal of those goods.

Economy: What human beings do. The activity of managing resources and producing, distributing, and consuming goods and services.

Ecosystem: A dynamic complex of plant, animal, fungal and microorganism communities and their associated non-living environment interacting as an ecological unit.

Eco-tourism: According to the US-based Eco-tourism Society, Responsible travel to natural areas which conserves the environment and sustains the livelihood of local people.

Eco-tourism activities: Activities included in a tour that are designed to entertain clients and are coordinated by a professional guide or interpreter. Over 80 activities have been listed for eco-tourism, such as birdwatching, hiking, diving, kayaking, participating in cultural events, photography, and mountaineering.

Eco-tourism product: A combination of resources, activities, and services, which are sold and managed through professional tour operators.

Eco-tourism resources: Natural and cultural features that attract visitors, such as landscapes, endemic or rare flora and fauna, cultural festivals, and historical monuments.

Eco-tourism services: Tourism services such as transportation, food, lodging, guiding and interpretation services which cause minimal damage to the biological and cultural environments and promote a better understanding of the natural and cultural history of an area.

Endangered species: Species of plants or animals threatened with extinction because their numbers have declined to a critical level as a result of overharvesting or because their habitat has drastically changed. That critical level is the minimum viable population (MVP), and represents the smallest number of breeding pairs required to maintain the viability of species.

Endemism: The level of species that occur naturally only in a specific region or site.

Environment: A combination of the various physical and biological elements that affect the life of an organism. Although it is common to refer to 'the' environment, there are in fact many environments eg, aquatic or terrestrial, microscopic to global, all capable of change in time and place, but all intimately linked and in combination constituting the whole earth/atmosphere system.

Environmentally-sound: The maintenance of a healthy environment and the protection of life-sustaining ecological processes. It is based on thorough knowledge and requires or will result in products, manufacturing processes, developments, etc. which are in harmony with essential ecological processes and human health.

Escort: A person, usually employed by a tour operator, who accompanies a tour from departure to return as a guide or troubleshooter; or a person who performs such functions only at the destination. The terms host-escort or host are often used, and are preferred, to describe this service.

Escorted Tour: A pre-arranged travel program, usually for a group, with host service. Fully escorted tours also may use local guide services.

Fair trade: Equitable, non-exploitative trade between developing world suppliers and Western consumers.

Fam Tour: A complimentary or reduced-rate travel program for travel agents, airline and rail employees, or other travel buyers, designed to acquaint participants with specific destinations and to stimulate the sale of travel. Familiarization tours are sometimes offered to journalists as research trips for the purpose of cultivating media coverage of specific travel products.

First Nations: A collective term for the original, pre-European inhabitants of the US, Canada, Hawaii, Australia and New Zealand. In individual countries, different terms are sometimes used, for example, Aboriginal, indigenous, tribal, Indian, First Peoples, Native American, AmerIndian.

Foreign Independent Travel or Foreign Individual Travel (FIT): An international pre-paid, unescorted tour that includes several travel elements such as accommodations, rental cars and sightseeing. A FIT operator specializes in preparing FITs documents at the request of retail travel agents. FITs usually receive travel vouchers to present to on-site services as verification of pre-payment.

Geotourism: Focuses on preserving a destination's geographic "character"-the combination of natural and human attributes that make one place distinct from another. Geotourism encompasses cultural and environmental concerns, as well as the local impact tourism has upon communities and their individual economies and lifestyles.

Green travel: A UK alternative to the American term eco-tourism.

Ground Operator: A company that provides local travel services, including transportation or guide services.

Historic District: A defined geographical area that may be as small as a few contiguous buildings, or as large as an entire neighborhood, business district, or community. Within this district are historic properties associated with a particular time or theme in a community's history. Often the collective significance of the district is greater than any one building or archaeological site.

Historic Property: A site with qualities that make it significant in history, architecture, archaeology, engineering or culture; sometimes more specifically a site that is eligible for or listed on the National Register of Historic Places, or on a local or state register of significant sites.

Hostel: An inexpensive, supervised lodging, particularly used by young people or elders.

Hotel Package: A sales device offered by a hotel, sometimes consisting of no more than a room and breakfast; sometimes, especially at resort hotels, consisting of ground transportation, room, meals, sports facilities and other components.

Incentive Tour: A trip offered as a prize, usually by a company, to stimulate employee sales or productivity.

Independent traveller: Someone who travels without booking a package tour.

Indigenous people: The original inhabitants of a country and their descendants. Indigenous communities are often, but not always, tribal peoples and the two terms are often and easily confused. See also First Nations, Aboriginal.

Local communities/people: People living in tourist destinations, especially in the rural developing world.

Multinational corporation: See transnational corporation.

National conservation strategies: Plans that highlight country-level environmental priorities and opportunities for sustainable management of natural resources, following the example of the World Conservation Strategy published by the World Conservation Union (IUCN) in 1980. Though governments may support preparation for the strategies, they are not bound to follow IUCN's recommendations.

Native Americans: A collective term for the indigenous people of the Americas. Also First Nations, AmerIndians, American Indians, Indians.

Net Rate: Price of goods to be marked up for eventual resale to the consumer.

NGO: Non-governmental organisation: an independent pressure group or campaigning organisation, usually non-profit.

Package tour: A holiday combining transport and accommodation in an inclusive price. Travel products offering an inclusive price with elements that would otherwise be purchased separately. Usually has a pre-determined price, length of time and features but can also offer options for separate purchase.

Packager: Anyone organizing a tour including prepaid transportation and travel services, usually to more than one destination.

Person-trip: The research term for one person taking one trip of 100 or more miles, one-way, away from home.

Preservation: The conservation of the qualities and materials that make historic buildings, sites, structures, objects and districts significant. Approaches to preservation include stabilization, restoration, rehabilitation, and reconstruction.

Proper resource pricing: The pricing of natural resources at levels which reflect their combined economic and environmental values.

Pro-poor tourism: Tourism that benefits poor people in developing-world tourist destinations

Rack Rate: The official cost posted by a hotel, attraction or rental car, but usually not used by tour operators.

Receptive Operator: A tour operator or travel agent specializing in services for incoming visitors, such as meeting them at the airport and facilitating their transfer to lodging facilities.

Responsible tourism: Tourism that aims to avoid harmful impacts on people and environments. Sometimes referred to as ethical tourism. Other similar concepts include People First Tourism, reality tourism, etc.

Retail Agency: Travel company selling directly to the public, sometimes a subdivision of a wholesale and/or retail travel organization.

Stakeholders: Individuals who have a vested interest in development, including community members; environmental, social, and community NGOs; natural resource, planning, and government officials; hotel owners, tour operators, guides, transportation providers, and representatives from other related services in the private sector.

Supplier: The producer of a unit of travel merchandise, such as a carrier, hotel, sightseeing operator, or cultural organization.

Sustainable development: Development that meets the needs and aspirations of the current generation without compromising the ability to meet those of future generations. It is widely accepted that achieving sustainable development requires balance between three dimensions of complementary change:

- Ecological (towards maintenance and restoration of healthy ecosystems)
- Social (towards poverty eradication and sustainable livelihoods)
- Economic (towards sustainable patterns of production and consumption)

Sustainable Tourism: Tourism that does not degrade the environment or local cultures/societies. The primary concern of sustainable tourism is to support balance within the ecological environment and minimize the impact upon it by mass-market tourism. The use of this term is evolving as it is also used to describe the impact of mass-tourism on cultural and historic resources.

Technical Visit: Tour designed for a special interest groups, usually to visit a place of business with a common interest. The tour usually includes part business/part leisure and is customized for the group.

Third World, the: Now generally referred to as either developing countries or *the South*.

Tour: Any prearranged (but not necessarily prepaid) journey to one or more places.

Tour Leader: A person with special qualifications to conduct a particular travel group, such as a botanist who conducts a garden tour.

Tour Operator: A company that creates and/or markets inclusive tours and/or performs tour services.

Tourists: Holiday-makers, mainly (but no longer exclusively) from the West. The term is sometimes used to distinguish package tourists from independent travellers, but can be used to mean anyone going on holiday.

Transnational corporation: Correctly, a large company with shareholders in more than one country. The term is often used more loosely to mean any large, powerful, Western-owned company.

Tribal peoples: People living in close-knit social units based on kinship ties and shared belief systems. While most remaining tribal communities are indigenous, not all indigenous peoples still live tribally. (On the other hand, for example, many 'hill-tribes' in northern Thailand migrated there fairly recently from southern China, making them tribal but not indigenous to Thailand.)

Vouchers: Documents issued by a tour operator to be exchanged for accommodations, meals, sightseeing, admission tickets, etc.

Wholesaler: A company that creates and markets inclusive tours and FITS for sale through travel agents. Company usually sells nothing at retail, and does not always create his/her own product. Company also is less likely to perform local services.

World Commission on Environment and Development: Established by the United Nations General Assembly in 1983 to examine international and global environmental problems and to propose strategies for sustainable development. Chaired by Norwegian Prime Minister Gro Harlem Brundtland, the independent commission held meetings and public hearing around the world and submitted a report on its inquiry to the General Assembly in 1987.

World Summit on Sustainable Development (WSSD): The World Summit on Sustainable Development takes place from

26 August - 4 September 2002 in Johannesburg, South Africa. Governments, UN agencies, and civil society organisations will come together to assess progress since the UN Conference on Environment and Development held in Rio in 1992 (hence the title 'Rio + 10' for the Johannesburg meeting). Sustainable development is defined in the report from the Rio meeting as being 'economic progress which meets all of our needs without leaving future generations with fewer resources than those we enjoy'.

World Tourism Organisation (WTO): A UN-affiliated organisation based in Madrid and comprising government and industry representatives, that compiles statistics and guidelines and promotes global tourism.

World Travel and Tourism Council (WTTC): An organisation based in Brussels and London and made up of the chief executives of the world's largest travel companies, that lobbies on behalf of the tourism industry.

Chapter 1

Global Tourism: A WTO Perspective on Sustainable Tourism

The World Tourism Organisation (WTO/OMT), a specialized agency of the United Nations, is the leading international organisation in the field of tourism. It serves as a global forum for tourism policy issues and practical source of tourism know-how.

With its headquarters in Madrid, Spain, the WTO plays a central and decisive role in promoting the development of responsible, sustainable and universally accessible tourism, with the aim of contributing to economic development, international understanding, peace, prosperity and universal respect for, and observance of, human rights and fundamental freedoms. In pursuing this aim, the Organisation pays particular attention to the interests of developing countries in the field of tourism.

The WTO plays a catalytic role in promoting technology transfers and international cooperation, in stimulating and developing public-private sector partnerships and in encouraging the implementation of the Global Code of Ethics for Tourism, with a view to ensuring that member countries, tourist destinations and businesses maximize the positive economic, social and cultural effects of tourism and fully reap its benefits, while minimizing its negative social and environmental impacts.

In 2005, the WTO's membership is comprised of 145 countries, seven territories and more than 300 Affiliate Members representing the private sector, educational institutions, tourism associations and local tourism authorities.

GLOBAL CODE OF ETHICS FOR TOURISM

Tourism for Prosperity and Peace

At the start of the new millennium, tourism is firmly established as the number one industry in many countries and the fastest-growing economic sector in terms of foreign exchange earnings and job creation.

International tourism is the world's largest export earner and an important factor in the balance of payments of most nations.

Tourism has become one of the world's most important sources of employment. It stimulates enormous investment in infrastructure, most of which also helps to improve the living conditions of local people. It provides governments with substantial tax revenues. Most new tourism jobs and business are created in developing countries, helping to equalize economic opportunities and keep rural residents from moving to overcrowded cities.

Intercultural awareness and personal friendships fostered through tourism are a powerful force for improving international understanding and contributing to peace among all the nations of the world.

The WTO recognizes that tourism can have a negative cultural, environmental and social impact if it is not responsibly planned, managed and monitored. The WTO thus encourages governments to play a vital role in tourism, in partnership with the private sector, local authorities and non-governmental organisations.

In its belief that tourism can be effectively used to address the problems of poverty, WTO made a commitment to contribute to the United Nations Millennium Development Goals through a new initiative to develop sustainable tourism as a force for poverty elimination. The programme, known as ST-EP (Sustainable Tourism-Eliminating Poverty), focuses the longstanding work of both organisations on encouraging sustainable tourism with a view to alleviating poverty and was implemented in 2003.

SUSTAINABLE DEVELOPMENT

More than 75 Years of Tourism Experience

The World Tourism Organisation had its beginnings as the International Congress of Official Tourist Traffic Associations set up in 1925 in the Hague. It was renamed the International Union of Official Travel Organisations (IUOTO) after World War II and moved to Geneva. IUOTO was a technical, non-governmental organisation, whose membership at its peak included 109 National Tourist Organisations (NTOs) and 88 Associate Members, among them private and public groups.

As tourism grew and became an integral part of the fabric of modern life, its international dimension increased and national governments started to play an increasingly important role-their activities covering the whole spectrum from infrastructure to regulations. By the mid-1960s, it became clear that there was a need for more effective tools to keep developments under review and to provide tourism with intergovernmental machinery especially equipped to deal with the movement of persons, tourism policies and tourism's impacts.

In 1967, the members of IUOTO called for its transformation into an intergovernmental body empowered to deal on a worldwide basis with all matters concerning tourism and to cooperate with other competent organisations, particularly those of the United Nations' system, such as the World Health Organisation (WHO), UNESCO, and the International Civil Aviation Organisation (ICAO).

A resolution to the same effect was passed in December 1969 by the UN General Assembly, which recognized the decisive and central role the transformed IUOTO should play in the field of world tourism in cooperation with the existing machinery within the UN. Following this resolution, the WTO's Statutes were ratified in 1974 by the States whose official tourist organisations were members of IUOTO.

Thus IUOTO became the World Tourism Organisation (WTO) and its first General Assembly was held in Madrid in

May 1975. The Secretariat was installed in Madrid early the following year at the invitation of the Spanish Government, which provides a building for the Headquarters.

In 1976, WTO became an executing agency of the United Nations Development Programme (UNDP) and in 1977, a formal cooperation agreement was signed with the United Nations itself. In 2003, the WTO was converted into a specialized agency of the United Nations and reaffirmed its leading role in international tourism.

Since its early years, WTO's membership and influence in world tourism have continued to grow. By 2005, its membership included 145 countries, seven territories and some 350 Affiliate Members, representing the private sector, educational institutions, tourism associations and local tourism authorities.

Key Events

1925	International Congress of Official Tourist Traffic Associations, The Hague, The Netherlands
1934	Creation of International Union of Official Tourist Propaganda Organisations (IUOTPO), The Hague, The Netherlands 1947 IUOTPO is converted to the International Union of Official Travel Organisations (IUOTO)
1969	Intergovernmental Conference in Sofia, Bulgaria and the UN General Assembly, call for creation of intergovernmental organisation on tourism
1970	In Mexico, on 27 September (future date of World Tourism Day) IUOTO's Extraordinary General Assembly adopts the Statutes of World Tourism Organisation
1975	First General Assembly of the World Tourism Organisation is held in Madrid, Spain and WTO is officially launched with Robert Lonati (France) as Secretary-General

1976	WTO Secretariat moves from Geneva to Madrid
1977/1979	WTO General Assembly held in Torremolinos, Spain
1979	"World Tourism Day" created, to be celebrated every year on 27th September
1980	WTO convenes World Tourism Conference in Manila; the Manila Declaration on World Tourism is unanimously adopted
1981	WTO General Assembly held in Rome, Italy
1982	World Tourism Conference convened in Acapulco; Acapulco Document is adopted
1983	WTO General Assembly held in New Delhi, India
1985	Tourism Bill of Rights and Tourist Code adopted at WTO General Assembly, Sofia, Bulgaria
1986	Willibald Pahr (Austria) elected Secretary-General
1987	WTO General Assembly held in Madrid, Spain
1989	WTO General Assembly held in Paris, France
1989	Inter-Parliamentary Conference on Tourism, jointly organised with the Inter-Parliamentary Union, adopts The Hague Declaration on Tourism
1990	Antonio Enríquez Savignac (Mexico) elected Secretary-General
1991	WTO General Assembly held in Buenos Aires, Argentina
1993	WTO General Assembly held in Bali, Indonesia
1995	WTO General Assembly held in Cairo, Egypt
1996	Francesco Frangialli (France) appointed interim Secretary-General after Antonio Enríquez Savignac's early retirement
1996	Second WTO Forum on Parliaments and Local Authorities: Tourism Policy-Makers, adopts the Bali Declaration on Tourism, Indonesia

1997	WTO General Assembly held in Istanbul, Turkey
1997	Francesco Frangialli (France) elected Secretary-General
1999	WTO General Assembly held in Santiago, Chile
2001	Fourteenth General Assembly held jointly in Seoul, Republic of Korea and Osaka, Japan
2001	Francesco Frangialli (France) re-elected Secretary-General
2003	Transformation of the WTO into a UN specialized agency

WTO STATISTICS

The bodies of the World Tourism Organisation are the:

General Assembly

The General Assembly is the principal gathering of the World Tourism Organisation. It meets every two years to approve the budget and programme of work and to debate topics of vital importance to the tourism sector. Every four years it elects a Secretary-General. The General Assembly is composed of Full Members and Associate Members. Affiliate Members and representatives of other international organisations participate as observers.

Executive Council

The Executive Council is WTO's governing board, responsible for ensuring that the Organisation carries out its work and adheres to its budget. It meets twice a year and is composed of 29 Members elected by the General Assembly in a ratio of one for every five Full Members. As host country of WTO's Headquarters, Spain has a permanent seat on the Executive Council. Representatives of the Associate Members and Affiliate Members participate in Executive Council meetings as observers.

Regional Commissions

WTO has six regional commissions-Africa, the Americas, East Asia and the Pacific, Europe, the Middle East and South Asia. The commissions meet at least once a year and are composed of all the Full Members and Associate Members from that region. Affiliate Members from the region participate as observers.

Committees

Specialized committees of WTO Members advise on management and programme content. These include: the Programme Committee, the Committee on Budget and Finance, the Committee on Statistics and Macroeconomic Analysis of Tourism, the Committee on Market Intelligence and Promotion, the Sustainable Development of Tourism Committee, the Quality Support Committee, the WTO Education Council, the WTO Business Council and the World Committee on Tourism Ethics.

Secretariat

The Secretariat is led by Secretary-General Francesco Frangialli of France, who supervises about 90 full-time staff at WTO's Madrid Headquarters. He is assisted by the Deputy Secretary-General Dawid de Villiers of South Africa. These officials are responsible for implementing WTO's programme of work and serving the needs of Members. The WTO Business Council is supported by a full-time Chief Executive Officer at the Madrid Headquarters, a position that is financed by the Spanish Government. The Secretariat also includes a regional support office for Asia-Pacific in Osaka, Japan, financed by the Japanese Government. The official languages of WTO are English, Spanish, French, Russian and Arabic.

COOPERATION FOR DEVELOPMENT OF MARKET INTELLIGENCE

Shared Technical Skills

The transfer of tourism know-how to developing countries is one of the World Tourism Organisation's fundamental tasks. As an executing agency of the United Nations Development Programme, WTO contributes decades of experience in tourism to the sustainable development goals of nations throughout the world.

Acting on requests from Member States, WTO secures financing, locates the world's leading experts, and carries out a gamut of development projects-large and small. Long-term projects have included:

- Tourism Master Plan for Pakistan (2001).
- Tourism Master Plans for eight Chinese provinces (2000-2002).
- Development of national parks in Rwanda (1999).
- Tourism development strategy for Moldova (1999-ongoing).
- Integrated development programme for Palestinian Authority (2000).
- Development activities in some 70 countries worth more than US $2.5 million (2001-2002).

Projects can also be short and targeted to address an immediate need, for example:

- Tourism legislation in Syria.
- Eco-tourism plan for Lithuania.
- Statistics development in Botswana.
- Social impact study for the Maldives.
- Management of heritage sites in Ecuador.
- Hotel classification for Bolivia.

- Women's empowerment plan for Namibia.
- Training for quality service in tourism in Peru.

Tourism has proven to be a powerful tool in alleviating poverty. It has become the economic mainstay of many of the world's least developed countries (LDCs), providing them with one of the opportunities for development and job creation. A joint programme with UNCTAD called Sustainable Tourism Eliminating Poverty (STEP) focuses on the twin subjects of sustainable tourism and alleviation of poverty, in order to increase their potential synergies and contribute more strongly to sustainable development in least developed and developing countries. STEP was launched at WSSD in Johannesburg in August 2002.

REGIONAL ACTIVITIES COMMUNICATIONS

Around the World

Direct actions that strengthen and support the efforts of National Tourism Administrations are carried out by WTO's regional representatives.

Each region of the world—Africa, the Americas, East Asia and the Pacific, Europe, the Middle East and South Asia— receives special attention from its regional representative based at the Headquarters of the World Tourism Organisation in Madrid.

Regional representatives are WTO's front line of contact with member countries. They are constantly on the go, but regional representatives are much more than travelling ambassadors.

They meet with the top tourism officials from each of the countries in their region to analyse problems and offer solutions.

To create specific development projects, they act as a liaison between tourism authorities and financing sources, especially the United Nations Development Programme.

They represent WTO at national and regional tourism events.

They organize national seminars on topics of particular relevance to an individual country.

They hold regional conferences on problems that are shared by many countries so that Members can exchange experiences and work towards common goals. Recent conferences have been held on the Challenge of Globalization in the Middle East, Human Resource Development in East Asia and the Pacific, the Euro and Tourism in Europe and Quality Standards in the Americas region, Crisis Management in East Asia and the Pacific, etc.

They help facilitate productive contacts between tourism authorities and other branches of government—often at the presidential level. All of these activities are designed to help increase the stature of National Tourism Administrations within their own country, while at the same time building awareness of new developments in tourism and improving technical, operational skills.

In a special effort to help boost tourism to sub-Saharan Africa, WTO has developed a specific programme of technical activities for the years 2003-2004.

WTO's six Regional Commissions meet at least once a year to discuss the Organisation's activities and set priorities for the future. Affiliate Members from the region are encouraged to participate in the meetings and seminars.

Regional Promotion Projects WTO is in a unique position to carry out special projects that promote tourism to a group of Member States. The Silk Road and the Slave Route are two of these projects, initiated in cooperation with the United Nations Scientific and Cultural Organisation (UNESCO).

The Silk Road Project, launched in 1994, aims at revitalizing the ancient highways used by Marco Polo through tourism. The Silk Road stretches 12,000 km from Asia to Europe and 22 countries have joined forces for this project: Armenia, Azerbaijan, China, DPR Korea, Egypt, Georgia, Greece, Islamic

Republic of Iran, Italy, Israel, Japan, Kazakhstan, Kyrgyzstan, Mongolia, Pakistan, Republic of Korea, Russian Federation, Syrian Arab Republic, Tajikistan, Turkmenistan, Turkey and Uzbekistan. Joint promotional activities include seminars, a brochure and a video.

The Slave Route Project, initiated in 1995 as part of the United Nations' International Year of Tolerance, aims to boost tourism to western African nations. Its immediate goals are to restore monuments, enhance history museums and launch joint information campaigns in selected tourism generating markets, which will motivate foreign visitors to learn about the history of these countries and to discover their roots.

World Tourism Day

Since 1980, Members of the World Tourism Organisation have been celebrating World Tourism Day every year on September 27th. Events include parades, concerts, tourism fairs, seminars, dinners, dances, and free entrance to museums-anything and everything that draws attention to the important role that tourism plays in the local community.

Task Force for Destination Management

To reflect the growing decentralization of tourism administration, WTO formed a task force to focus on issues that are of special concern at the destination level. Some concerns of the task force include: management of congestion at coastal destinations; economic measurement of tourism at the local level; destination marketing for cities; information and communication technologies; human resource development; and risk and crisis management at individual tourism destinations. The Task Force for Destination Management meets periodically and acts as an informal advisory body of WTO, with the aim of encouraging new work in these areas and identifying ongoing WTO projects that are relevant to tourism officials working in destination management.

Business Council Publications

Hand-in-Hand with the private sector WTO is unique among international intergovernmental organisations in that it is open to membership by the operating sector and promotes various methods of cooperation amongst its Members. Airlines, hotel chains, tour operators, trade associations, consultants, promotion boards and educational institutions make up approximately 350 Members of the WTO Business Council (WTOBC).

WTOBC utilizes a partnership approach to tourism as a method to promote public and private integration and as a model of understanding between the two sectors. To achieve their objectives, WTOBC aids Members in expanding their tourism businesses through industry networking, forming contacts with the necessary government officials strengthening industry-education relationship, and conducting specialized research projects of the private sector.

Currently, the WTOBC is undertaking numerous projects with the hope of creating more public-private partnerships and sustained cooperation amongst tourism industries. These projects include investigations into the factors that affect tourism, methods of managing congestion on sites, assisting small and medium size enterprises, and implementing new technology.

Under the guidance of its Board of Directors, WTOBC continues their research on the above-mentioned Projects accompanied by annual studies, data compilation, research publication and organisation of conferences. The Council continues to promote integration between public and private sectors with themes that are of special interest to the business community which include:

- Public-Private Sector Cooperation—Enhancing Tourism Competitiveness
- Marketing Tourism Destinations Online—Strategies for the Information Age

- E-Business for Tourism
- Tourism Taxation—Striking a Fair Deal
- Changes in Leisure Time

TOURISM AND TECHNOLOGY DOCUMENTATION

The Internet and other computer technologies are revolutionizing the way tourism business is conducted and the way destinations are promoted. WTO's work in the area of new Information Technologies (IT) aims to provide leadership in the field of IT and tourism, as well as helping to bridge the digital divide between the have and have-nots among WTO's membership.

WTO carries out new research and studies of IT in connection with the promotion and development of tourism, such as the publications Marketing Tourism Destinations Online and E-Business for Tourism. It communicates the content of these studies throughout the world in a series of regional seminars.

WTO also operates a Strategic Advisory Board on IT and Tourism that brings together a small number of high-level experts from destinations, private businesses and researchers.

Tourism technology is especially suited to cooperation projects between the public and private sectors. The objective is to keep all members up-to-date on the constantly changing technologies that will affect the tourism industry in the years to come.

JOINING THE WORLD TOURISM ORGANISATION

Leadership in Tourism Education

WTO.HRD The WTO Human Resource Development Department (WTO.HRD) works to add value to the tourism sector of WTO Member States improving their capacity building and providing direct support in tourism education, training and knowledge. The WTO.HRD coordinates the activities of the WTO Education Council as well as those of the WTO.Themis Foundation with the common goal of achieving the tourism competitiveness and sustainability of WTO Members through excellence in tourism education.

Its mission is to build the knowledge capacity of WTO Members, providing leadership, initiative and coordination in quality tourism education, training and research through public-private partnerships among institutions and WTO Member States. More information

WTO Themis Foundation

Based in Andorra and generously sponsored by its Government, the WTO.Themis Foundation provides the administrative back-up to WTO.HRD to develop and disseminate tourism education, training and knowledge products, thus optimising service to WTO Members.

Its mission is to promote quality and efficiency in tourism education and training in close coordination with WTO and its Human Resource Development Department (WTO.HRD), facilitating administration and management in implementing its programme of work and enlarging the scope of services to WTO Members. More information

WTO Education Council

The WTO Education Council (WTO.EdC) is made up of leading tourism education, training and research institutions as well as business schools worldwide that have obtained the WTO.TedQual Certification for at least one of their tourism education programmes. With over 100 members, it forms a chapter of the WTO Affiliate Members, and is well represented in the Board of the Affiliates, their decision-making body. The WTO.EdC is an active agent within WTO and in the development and implementation of the WTO.HRD Programme of Work. More information

The main human resource development products are:

- *WTO TedQual*: A framework of programmes for quality in tourism education. The WTO.TedQual Certification is granted to training and education institutions by means of a quality audit. The TedQual institutions can request membership in the WTO Education Council (Affiliate Members). There are also TedQual Seminars (Educating the Educators) for Member States and TedQual Consulting on quality issues for education and training centres.

- *WTO Practicum*: This is a biannual programme for officials from WTO Member States. It is carried out at WTO Headquarters for a period of two weeks and includes GTAT.TPS seminars, workshops, technical visits and working meetings with the responsible staff of the Organisation.

- *WTO Themis TedQual Practicum*: A practicum programme designed especially for officials from WTO Member States who are proposed by their Governments as liaisons with WTO in matters of education and training.

- *WTO GTAT*: A set of programmes (General Tourism Achievement Test) designed to improve the performance of teaching and learning in tourism. These include software for examinations and course development and implementation, GTAT Courses to improve specific knowledge and/or prepare for exams, GTAT Diagnosis to ascertain strong and weak points in specific subjects, GTAT Exams and GTAT Certification of Proficiency for students and tourism professionals.

- *WTO Sbest Initiative*: A framework for a range of WTO Programmes aimed at contributing to excellence in destinations and tourism companies through quality training and education. Programmes include the WTO.Sbest Training, WTO.Sbest Audit and WTO Tourism Labour Market Observatory. Institutions, companies and destinations satisfactorily completing these programmes receive WTO.Sbest Awards. Many of these programmes are executed in coordination with the WTO Destination Management Task Force.

■ *WTO Tourism Labour Market Observatory*: This programme was recently initiated by the WTO Education Council in conjunction with WTO.HRD and the WTO Destination Management Task Force. Its objective is to obtain quantitative and qualitative information on tourism labour markets in key destinations worldwide through panels of employers, workers, consumers and students. This is coordinated through WTO.Sbest tourism destinations and WTO TedQual Centres.

Other products:

■ WTO.SIS Seminars;
■ Publications;
■ WTO.TedProm;
■ WTO Ulysses Awards for Innovation and the Application of Knowledge in Tourism; and
■ Annual WTO.EdC Conference.

Quality and Trade: in search of common denominators, fairness and transparency

This activity follows the previous programme on Quality in Tourism Development. With an increased focus on the economics of tourism, trade and the enterprise it seeks to assist government and private sector Members in determining and pursuing quality-related objectives, standards and measures as a contribution to sustainable development and poverty alleviation.

The following specific areas are covered:

■ Trade in tourism services, including access to tourism markets, competition and globalization.

- Safety and security, including health issues.
- Guidance, harmonization and recognition of quality-related standards.

Reference to standards is present in all these areas. On trade issues, WTO works closely with the United Nations Conference on Trade and Development (UNCTAD) and with the World Trade Organisation (WTO-OMC). The aim is to relate tourism policies and strategies to multilateral negotiations according to the General Agreement on Trade in Services (GATS) designed to achieve progressively higher levels of liberalization with a view to promoting economic growth and the development of developing countries. Briefings and debate on trade in tourism are held periodically to help Members carry out comprehensive and informed trade policies.

The inclusion of the safety and security area is explained by it being considered as a fundamental quality factor. The current focus is on preparing a model work plan for tourism destinations based on objective safety and security criteria, a model code of conduct on travel advisories and a revised WTO document Health Information and Formalities in International Travel, to be submitted to the 16th session of the General Assembly in 2005 and taking stock of the new International Health Regulations of the World Health Organisation (IHR 2005).

Under the chapter of quality standards, the specific aims include guidance to Members undertaking tourism quality programmes, the design of standards based on common denominators and cultural diversity, a hotel classification guidance document, and contributions to the work of the International Organisation for Standardization (ISO) on tourism signs and symbols and other tourism related standards.

In relation to each area the Quality and Trade in Tourism department is also engaged in the preparation of "implementation parameters" for the Global Code of Ethics for Tourism. The operation of the Code and the secretariat of the

World Committee on Tourism Ethics are now dealt with by Sustainable Development of Tourism department.

Key Publications and Instruments

Tourism in the Least Developed Countries, GATS and Tourism, Tourist Safety and Security Tourism Signs and Symbols, Recommended Measures for Tourism Safety Health Information and Formalities in International Travel Creating Tourism Opportunities for the Handicapped WTO Statement against Organised Sex Tourism Quality, Hygiene and Safety of Food in the Tourism Sector

Global Code of Ethics for Tourism

Adopted by the WTO General Assembly in 1999 and acknowledged by the United Nations General Assembly in 2001 by a special resolution, the Code sets out a ten-point blueprint for safeguarding the resources upon which tourism depends and ensuring that its economic benefits are equitably shared.

The Code is based on the principles of sustainability that underpin all of WTO's programmes, with special emphasis on involving local communities in planning, managing and monitoring tourism development. It includes nine articles outlining the 'rules of the game' for destinations, governments, tour operators, travel agents, tourism workers and developers, and travelers themselves.

The tenth article involves implementation of the code through the activities of the World Committee on Tourism Ethics.

Sustainable Development

Ensuring the sustainable development and management of tourism so that its benefits can be enjoyed for generations to come is the philosophy behind the activities carried out by the

Sustainable Tourism Development Section. WTO creates practical instruments that allow tourism managers, in both the public and private sectors, to apply the principles of sustainability to concrete situations. The Section has issued several publications, manuals, inventories and analyses of best practices, which have been widely circulated and organised seminars have been held throughout the world. Some major projects include:

International Year of Eco-tourism 2002 Recognizing the global importance of eco-tourism, the United Nations designated the year 2002 as the International Year of Eco-tourism. A World Eco-tourism Summit in Quebec, Canada, (May 2002), jointly organised with the United Nations Environment Programme, gathered around 1,200 participants and resulted in the Quebec Declaration on Eco-tourism, containing 49 specific guidelines for sustainable eco-tourism development and management.

World Summit on Sustainable Development The World Tourism Organisation was actively involved in the preparations for the World Summit on Sustainable Development that took place in Johannesburg on 26 August—4 September 2002.

Planning for sustainable development of tourism WTO has published several manuals for tourism planning at the national, regional and local levels. It organizes national seminars on tourism planning for local authorities in developing countries.

Indicators of sustainable tourism Sustainable tourism indicators are fundamental tools for the planning and monitoring of tourism development. WTO has been involved in this area since 1992, conducting pilot studies, producing a manual and teaching how to use indicators through a series of regional technical workshops in different regions and types of destinations.

Good practices in sustainable development of tourism Providing successful examples of tourism development and management is an important way of disseminating experiences that can be adapted at other destinations. WTO has published three compilations of good practice cases in sustainable tourism, each of them containing around 50 case studies from more than 30 countries in a structured format.

Key Publications

- *Sustainable Development of Tourism*: Guide for Local Authorities, with three regional supplements (Africa, Americas, Asia and the Pacific).
- A Practical Guide to the Use of Sustainable Tourism Indicators.
- Agenda 21 for the Travel and Tourism Industry.
- Guidelines for the Development of National Parks and Protected Areas.
- Sustainable Development of Tourism—A Compilation of Good Practices.
- Sustainable Development of Eco-tourism—A Compilation of Good Practices.
- Voluntary Initiatives for Sustainable Tourism
- Series of eco-tourism market studies.

Statistics

Proving the economic impact of tourism with solid facts and figures is the goal of WTO's Section on Statistics and Economic Measurement of Tourism. It helped create the Tourism Satellite Account (TSA) and is now assisting governments implement this accurate system of measuring the demand and supply sides of tourism.

WTO sets international standards for tourism measurement and reporting. Its recommendations on tourism statistics were adopted by the United Nations in 1993, creating a common language of tourism statistics that allows destinations to compare their success with that of their competitors. In 2000, the United Nations approved the Tourism Satellite Account methodology, making tourism the world's first sector to have international standards for measuring its economic impacts in a credible way.

WTO also provides the world's most comprehensive tourism statistics. Member States, private tourism companies, consulting firms, universities and the media all recognize WTO as the world's most comprehensive and reliable source of global tourism statistics and forecasts. Tourism data collected from 190 countries around the world include: arrivals, receipts, overnight stays, mode of transport, length of stay, tourist spending, and origin of visitors.

Tourism Satellite Account

Endorsed by the United Nations Statistical Commission, the Tourism Satellite Account is a joint project of several intergovernmental bodies and industry representatives. It sets a series of global standards and definitions that measure the tourism industry's true contribution in terms of: percentage of GDP, direct tourism jobs and capital investment. In compliance with United Nations recommendations, it runs alongside the national accounts framework. It will provide internationally comparable data developed by a country's own statistical institutions. TSA also puts tourism for the first time on an equal footing with other, less diversified economic sectors. Developing TSA is an opportunity for defining cooperative work between National Tourism Administrations, National Statistical Offices and Central Banks. Key publications:

- Compendium of Tourism Statistics.
- Yearbook of Tourism Statistics.
- Tourism Satellite Acount as an ongoing process: past, present and future developments.
- Enzo Paci Papers on Measuring the Economic Significance of Tourism, Vol. 1 and 2.
- Measuring Visitor Expendituer for Inbound Tourism.

Market Intelligence

Assisting governments and tourism professionals in understanding the constantly changing tourism marketplace is the aim of WTO's Section on Market Intelligence and Promotion. Identifying market trends as they are happening; short term and long-term forecasting; analyzing the world's generating markets; conducting research into niche markets; and providing evaluation tools for promotional campaigns are just some of the activities carried out each year.

The annual series of Tourism Market Trends reports provides a timely and comprehensive analysis of tourism results around the world. It enables tourism authorities to compare their performance to other countries of the same region, examining arrivals, receipts and the main factors affecting growth in the previous season.

Special attention is paid to studying tourism products, such as sports, cruises, MICE tourism (meetings, incentives, congresses and exhibitions) and market segments, such as eco-tourism, youth or senior tourism. Another important task is the analysis of outbound tourism of both consolidated and emerging markets. Research can be initiated in any specific topics relevant for tourism development. For instance, to increase insight in the evolution of the tourism sector, it was studied how consolidation by means of alliances, mergers and acquisitions in the sub-sectors of accommodation, air transport and distribution is impacting destinations, travel agents, small businesses and the consumer.

To assist Member States with tourism promotion, the Section conducts periodic surveys on tourism budgets and sources of financing. It also provides practical guidance whenever pertinent. For instance, after the September 11th attacks it monitored the subsequent situation of uncertainty, studied lessons learned from past crises and helped Members with strategies to adapt to sudden change in market conditions.

WTO's seven-volume forecast Tourism 2020 Vision on worldwide forecasts is a landmark study based on data gathered from Member States and interviews with over 75 tourism visionaries about the future of the industry. It predicts that international tourist arrivals will grow by an average of 4.1 per cent annually for the 25-year period 1995-2020. Tourism 2020 Vision includes forecasts of inbound and outbound tourism growth for countries in every region of the world and examines the outlook for several market segments.

Results are disseminated in various ways, such as through presentations and seminars, the WTO website and in a broad range of publications, including:

- Tourism Market Trends—five regional volumes and a world volume.
- Tourism Highlights.
- Tourism 2020 Vision—six regional volumes and a world volume.
- Budgets of National Tourism Administrations.
- Tourism Generating Markets.
- World Tourism Barometer.

Communications: A Focal Point for Tourism Information

Increasing awareness of the importance of tourism, promoting the WTO's work and objectives through effective communication in order to provide transparency of its activities, helping achieve the goals of all sections and keeping you informed about new projects, studies, seminar results and upcoming WTO activities are the primary goals of WTO's Press and Communications Section.

Members receive the WTO News, published quarterly, and the electronic Members' Update, published fortnightly. Non-members are reached through the media. The Press and Communications Section maintains a database of 2,000 key journalists around the world and contacts them regularly through news releases and press conferences.

The entire tourism industry is reached by WTO's website on the Internet and through major international tourism trade fairs where WTO operates an information booth, including:

- FITUR, Madrid
- ITB, Berlin
- MITT, Moscow
- WTM, London

Improving the promotional efforts of Member States through effective media relations, organizing press trips and seminars on media relations and crisis management, are even more goals of WTO's Press and Communications Section. It publishes Shining in the Media Spotlight, a communications manual that includes a directory of major media in the world's top tourism generating markets. The World Conference on Tourism Communications (TOURCOM), to be held in early 2004, will become a regular meeting place of tourism professionals from both, public and private sectors, with the international media.

Completely renovated in 2001, WTO's popular website on the Internet is available in English, French and Spanish, with a growing section in Russian and—to follow—in Arabic. The attractive homepage offers the latest news from WTO and easy-to-use links to all activities and products. Users have access to basic statistics on world tourism, seminars' programmes, a complete calendar of worldwide tourism events, details on special programmes such as the meetings of the Tourism Recovery Committee, the Silk Road Project, Protection of Children from Sexual Exploitation in Tourism and Sustainable Tourism—Eliminating Poverty (ST-EP).

Publications

One of WTO's most important functions is to serve as a permanent source of information for its Members and the world community. WTO fulfils this task in part through its extensive programme of publications and the new programme of electronic products. The broad span of these products corresponds to the vast sweep both of the Organisation's concerns and of the needs of its Members.

Today, WTO has already more than 250 titles available. Every year this list is extended by some 30 to 40 new titles in up to four official languages which are produced by the WTO publications department together with the originating sections. The Publications department runs at WTO headquarters in Madrid a bookshop from which all publications and electronic products can be ordered. Besides, all books and electronic products are displayed in a very detailed form and with excerpts in the WTO Infoshop at www.world-tourism.org/infoshop. Easy purchase and credit card payment options are just some of the comfortable features the shop offers. All products can also be ordered directly from a world-wide network of local distributors.

With the aim of improving the dissemination of our information as much as possible, translation and reproduction rights are also available to editorials that wish to publish WTO publications into other official and non-official languages. Until today WTO publications have been translated into more than 30 different languages.

With its recently launched Depository Library Programme, the WTO publications section encourages libraries to collect all WTO publications and make them available to a wider audience. All libraries which are complying with the requirements for Depositary Libraries are invited to share this initiative and are offered interesting financial conditions.

WTO aims to expand the scope, coverage, and quality of our publications and electronic products, as well as the number of editions available in English, French, Spanish, Russian and other languages. The Secretariat always welcomes feedback about any WTO product.

Documentation With the goal of acting as a true clearing-house, the WTO Documentation Centre endeavours to provide up to date qualitative information on tourism activities and related components on a theme-oriented basis.

The Documentation Centre concentrates its efforts to improve the information linkage networking between itself, WTO Members and other institutional partners, so as to facilitate tourism information access, transfer and exchange worldwide.

With these objectives in mind, the Centre offers online access to a tourism legislation database (LEXTOUR) providing bibliographic and textual data on laws and regulations existing both at the WTO Secretariat and in similar external legislative information systems.

As visible output products, the Centre delivers regular research reports on strategic issues, such as the role, spheres of competence and activities of tourism administrations and tourism investment policies. It also collaborates with other departments within the Secretariat in establishing a permanent tourism taxation monitoring information system.

To consolidate its function as a referral service, a specific database administrated by the Centre disseminates factual data on national and international tourism information holders and brokers (INFODOCTOUR) via the WTO Website. In addition, the Documentation Centre provides an authoritative tool for indexing and retrieving information on tourism and allied fields with the Multilingual Thesaurus on Tourism and Leisure Activities.

Who can join the World Tourism Organisation? WTO has three categories of membership: Full Members, Associate Members and Affiliate Members.

Full Membership is Open to All Sovereign States

Associate membership is open to territories not responsible for their external relations. Membership requires the prior approval of the government which assumes responsibility for their external relations.

Affiliate membership comprises a wide range of organisations and companies working directly in travel, tourism and related sectors. These may include: airlines and other transport, hotels and restaurants, tour operators and travel agents, banking institutions, insurance companies, travel assistance, publishing groups, etc. Affiliate membership is made up of three groups, the WTO Business Council, the WTO Education Council and the WTO Task Force on Destination Management. Affiliate membership requires endorsement by the government of the state in which the headquarters of the applicant is located. WTO is the only intergovernmental organisation that offers membership to the operational sector and in this way offers a unique contact point for discussion between government officials and industry leaders. WTO's broad-based Affiliate membership also has its own programme of activities which includes regular meetings and technical seminars on specific study topics.

SUSTAINABLE TOURISM: A NON-GOVERNMENTAL ORGANIZATION PERSPECTIVE

Introduction

Tourism is a rapidly growing phenomenon and has become one of the largest industries in the world. The impact of tourism is extremely varied. On one hand, it plays an important and certainly positive role in the socio-economic and political development in destination countries by, for instance, offering new employment opportunities. Also, in certain instances, it may contribute to a broader cultural understanding by creating awareness, respecting the diversity of cultures and ways of life. On the other hand, as a tool to create jobs, it has not fulfilled its expectations. At the same time, complaints from tourist destinations concerning massive negative impacts upon environment, culture and residents' ways of life have given rise to a demand for a more sustainable development in tourism. Different parties will have to be involved in the process of developing sustainable tourism. This section focuses on what the tourism industry itself can do in order to increase its sustainability, defines three major problems, and suggests possible tourism initiatives to help solve these problems. Other problems should also be included in the discussion for it to become exhaustive.

Industry Initiatives for Sustainable Tourism

Problems

Decreased Access to Natural Resources for the Local Communities and Environmental Degradation

Tourism is not, as many people assert, a clean and non-polluting industry. A major problem is the lack of a common understanding of what sustainable tourism or "eco-tourism" means. This ambiguity leads to violations of environmental regulations and standards. Hence, the environmental problems evolving from tourism are manifold. First of all, the tourism industry is very resource and land intensive. Consequently, the interest of the tourism sector will often be in conflict with local resource and land use practices. The introduction of tourism will imply an increased stress on resources available. An influx of tourists into the area will lead to a competition for resources. Employees working at the tourist sites compound this competition. Almost as a rule, tourists are supplied at the expense of the local population.

Tourist activities imply an intensified utilisation of vulnerable habitats. Investors and tourists do not necessarily possess awareness on how to use natural resources sustainably, and subsequently this utilisation often leads to a degradation of resources. Tourism is also a major generator of wastes. In most tourist regions of developing countries, sewage, wastewater and solid waste disposal are not properly managed or planned. Lastly, tourism is also responsible for a considerable proportion of increased volumes and mileage in global transport and hence the associated environmentally damaging pollutant emissions. The tourism industry has not shown sufficient willingness to (internalise or) compensate the cost of conservation of bio-diversity in, for instance, protected areas, even though they can profit from it.

Increasing Cultural Erosion and Disrespect for Human Rights

Tourism is a powerful agent of change. International tourism acts as a catalyst for the transition from traditional ways of life to so-called modern, Western forms of society. Accordingly, tourism often brings with it the introduction of new behaviour trends and norms. Very often, these are contrary to traditional norms existing in the host community, and can come into conflict with its cultural identity and threaten the traditional value systems there. The problem is that the investors seem to have a lack of cultural understanding of the invested society. There is a need for an increased awareness that establishment of new hotels etc. will have its consequences on the society and the people who live in it.

Tourism has become associated with violation of human rights. Many destination countries have experienced an increase in criminality, prostitution, alcohol and drug abuse as a consequence of tourism. Furthermore, child labour is commonplace in the tourism industry (particularly in the informal sector). According to estimates made by ILO (International Labour Organisation), between 3 and 19 million children and teenagers work in the tourism sector. A particularly abominable form of violation of human rights is child slavery and despicable abuse of children taking place in the booming sex industry in many countries. In these countries, tourism has led to an incredible increase in prostitution and also in the exploitation of children. The tourism industry has not yet come up with a general condemnation of these violations of human rights.

Unqualified Jobs and Foreign Exchange Leakage

The tourism industry is characterised by a high degree of monopoly, which implies a concentration of services and profits into very few big transnational corporations. In many countries, tourism facilities mostly belong to foreigners. Furthermore, in local host communities in many countries a relatively small number of people are involved in the tourism industry in host communities in many developing countries. Very often, there is a lack of qualified manpower in the locality. Hence, most employees are recruited form the big cities, neighbouring countries or even from the country of origin of the investors.

Multiplier effects from tourism are less significant than is often assumed. One reason is that tourism industries purchase most of their inputs (materials, products or services) in their country of origin. As a result, a considerable amount of foreign exchange revenues leaks from the destination countries. The more goods, services, physical capital and human capital a country must import for its tourism services, the higher the leakage. Very often the investors are not approaching the local community to see what it actually can provide. In addition to this, the General Agreement on Trade in Services (GATS), with its liberalisation of global trade and services, is increasingly undermining the possibilities of individual countries and regions to control their tourism industries and the possible economic gains from tourism.

Solutions

Decreased Access to Natural Resources for the Local Communities and Environmental Degradation

In general, the tourism industry should engage in promoting sustainability as a hallmark for investors. More specifically, investors in tourism should strive to adopt environmentally sound technologies or other measures to minimise the consumption of local ground water. In the case of water utilisation, such measures might be water saving equipment, desalination systems and collecting and utilising rainwater. Using other types of resources in a sustainable manner is, of course, also crucial. There is a need to use ecological materials and installation of renewable sources of energy systems (solar energy) in all new buildings and new construction. Furthermore there should be an acceleration of installation or solar/wind power in all public work projects of communities where tourism will be introduced. To prevent or minimise the impact of chemical inputs in soil, water and health, one should start utilising sound ecological methods, including IPM (Integrated Pest Management). Ecological methods need to be applied in all areas utilised for tourism, including in the maintenance of golf courts, gardens and recreational facilities.

Pollution of ground and coastal waters must be prevented, and recommendations must be made (perhaps even legislation) for tourism investors to invest in proper sewage treatment facilities. Appropriate waste disposal systems and ways to separate garbage into organic and non-organic waste should be developed. Organic waste can be composted and possibly reused on hotel gardens or even for local farming. This could be done through collaboration with local residents. Residents could organise themselves and manage the allocated dumping sites, and hence benefit from the system in receiving payment from the hotel for services rendered. A system to separate the different materials, and recycle some should be in place at the landfill site, thus reducing the waste even further.

To avoid degradation of the natural environment, tourism projects can help finance protected areas and safeguard ecologically sensitive regions against further environmental deterioration. By empowering local populations and have them participating in the entire process, sustainability will be ensured as it becomes accepted by and adjusted to the local communities. Also, a protected area might certainly be a suitable tourist-attraction, where tourists can experience amazing nature and learn about conservation and traditional uses of natural resources in the area.

Investors in tourism should always respect the traditional land tenure system in the area and the traditional user-right systems of resources. In regard to this, the communication and consultation with the local communities about resource-use is important. Tourism investors should not exclude local people from using local resources, and thus take away what they depend on for maintaining their well being. The tourism industry can and must take initiatives to implement that polluter(s) pay a principle (or other forms of internalisation of externalities) for pollution related to tourism operations. This may be organised and carried out through local tax systems or through funds established by the tourism industry for local community development. However, the paid principle should be applied for minor pollution only and should not be developed into a possibility for investors to pay a symbolic fine for imposed irreversible negative impacts on the local environment.

Inaccurate and/or mild environmental legislation in destination countries may possibly attract more foreign investors contributing to fast economic growth and development, but with environmental damage as a consequence. To avoid the dilemma, destination countries will have to choose between economic development and environmental protection international. Multinational enterprises must be committed to follow the environmental standards of their home country should these be stricter than those at the destinations.

Increasing Cultural Erosion and Disrespect for Human Rights

The tourism industry should promote projects, which are compatible with the cultural identity of the local population's way of life. Furthermore, the tourism sector should always make sure it acts in accordance with the cultural heritage, and respect the cultural integrity of tourism destinations. This might be accomplished by defining codes of conduct for the industry and hence providing investors with a checklist for sustainable tourism projects.

Establishing and developing tourist training programmes could be one way of managing codes of conducts for the tourists. Here, tourists can be informed and educated about the destination for their travel both before and after their arrival at the site. At the site, tourist information centres can be established through funding from the investor. The information given to tourists should include codes of conduct regarding appropriate behaviour and clothing. It is reasonable to assume that people's offending behaviour is largely a consequence of ignorance rather than intention. Consequently, information and facts about the destination, ways of life, history, cultural heritage is crucial to help tourists get along.

It is an absolute must that tourism investors do not engage in or promote child labour and prostitution. Moreover, it is appropriate that the industry commit themselves to a global campaign against such and any other violation of human rights. Evaluating the sustainability of the tourism development, in regards to cultural and human rights aspects, is highly recommended for those responsible for the tourism projects. As with the case mentioned earlier of preventing environmental degradation, this must be carried out through communication and consultation with the local communities.

Unqualified Jobs and Foreign Exchange Leakage

By devising local training programmes and establishing educational projects, the tourism industry can ensure that qualified local people are employed in their projects. One should train the local people instead of foreigners to become guides due to their knowledge of the area and resources. The investors should be responsive to the kind of knowledge, abilities and skills found in the local communities. Very often such knowledge and skills are well fitted to be used in tourist activities be it fishing trips, nature trails, souvenir sales or dancing courses for tourists etc.

To constrain foreign exchange leakage, those responsible for the tourism projects should ensure that local inputs are purchased for their projects. A proper examination of local resources available will be beneficial for both the industry and the local residents. Usually, there is considerable local willingness to start producing new products if a market for these products exists. The tourism sector should also adopt measures to prevent foreign exchange leakage by a commitment to re-investment of a fair share of the locally accrued profit. We have already mentioned protected areas, training programmes on codes of conduct for tourists, or possible training of local employees, as projects in need of funds. Initiatives towards more local community development projects should also be appropriate.

The tourism industry should promote the establishment of small and medium-sized tourism enterprises which, compared to large-scale hotels etc., have far more moderate impacts on the environment. It is the industry's responsibility to act as a model for communities to show that it is possible to do business whilst protecting natural resources. The industry should also promote and support local communities to start tourism-related businesses and grant access to low interest loans. It is the responsibility of the tourism sector to ensure total transparency in all transactions, and to prevent tourism projects from being used as projects for laundering illicit money, as well as to refuse using bribes as a means to obfuscate or avoid government rules and regulations. There should be a global boycott against those investors involved in such or other types of illegal activities.

General Recommendations and Possible Solutions which Concern all Three Problem Areas

Empowerment of residents at tourist destinations, through local participation, may be facilitated by providing written and legally binding contracts between local people and tourism investors. The contracts will help to avoid broken promises, which too many examples and previous experience prove to be a huge problem. In addition to the mentioned examples (providing proper information for tourists and establishing training programmes for residents), the tourism industry, through for instance the WTTC or the WTO with NGOs in the selection panels, could issue awards especially for sustainable tourism projects as an encouragement for investors.

Agents and Partnerships for Change

In this section, the focus has been on what the tourism industry itself can do in order to augment and improve its environmental, cultural, social and economic profile and make sure this is sustainable. However, the industry's effort cannot be successful without a profound collaboration with all stakeholders.

Within the industry, it is important that both small and large-scale tourism operators are included in the collaboration and that they participate in solving problems related to tourism development. As mentioned, a sustainable development of the tourism industry can only be ensured through participation of all local residents in the destination countries. There is a need for a willingness and ability for the partners to work with this kind of bottom-up approach. In this context, both environment and social NGOs have an important role to play, putting pressure on the industry and facilitating contracts and local participation for community development. Governments in both destination and countries of origin of tourists and investors are responsible for providing appropriate legislation for sustainable tourism development, and to follow up the tourism projects with sufficient monitoring and appropriate sanctioning. Exchange of successful experiences of sustainable tourism projects is an important factor in this connection. Lastly, an interdisciplinary approach to the problem is necessary: using local, regional and/or international consultative forums.

Influencing Consumer Behaviour to Promote Sustainable Tourism

Problems

International tourism plays an ambivalent role in contributing to cultural exchange and sustainable development. On the one hand, it involves a highly buffered, short-term consumer experience of other locales. Tourists can pay and leave, remaining isolated from negative impacts at the local level. On the other hand, tourism may increase recognition of the importance of respecting cultural diversity and developing an identity as a world citizen. It offers opportunities to educate consumers regarding responsible tourism and sustainable development. Consumers can play a major role in the transformation of societies towards sustainability. While mass tourism in the past was rather producer-driven, the industry today is becoming increasingly consumer-driven. In highly competitive tourism markets, well informed, responsible consumers can put increasing pressure on the industry to behave more responsibly.

A number of official proclamations have affirmed every individual's right to rest and leisure including tourism. However, tourism remains an unobtainable luxury for the majority of the world's population. Tourists primarily originate from affluent industrialised societies where tourism has become a mass phenomenon. Tourists' values, attitudes and behaviour are determined by their social environment, cultural identity and way of life which may be in conflict with local customs. Tourism is heterogeneous in nature, made up of many different types of traveller, seeking a wide range of tourism products. Demand is influenced by irrational factors, e.g. fashion and trends. Demand depends on the availability of time and money, on images, perceptions and attitudes. Tourists have various needs, desires and motivations, both of a 'push' and 'pull' nature. While household incomes in major tourist-sending countries are declining, industry sales projections continue to grow, indicating increasing competition. The consumer mind is set on discount prices and "buy now/pay later" options. This poses serious threats, as prices already lag far behind any realistic accounting of tourism costs and impacts.

Many of the demand patterns in tourism reflect the unsustainable lifestyles of industrialised consumer societies. Tourism acts as an agent in exporting these life-styles and consumerist attitudes to less industrialised societies via demonstration effects and modelling. Tourism increases demand for imported consumer goods in the destinations, with detrimental effects on the environment, due to the ecological costs of transport and the high amount of waste generated. Increasing imports also reduce local/national economic gains, due to foreign exchange leakage.

The over-consumption of resources by tourists and tourism infrastructure (e.g. the excessive use of water, firewood or food) is incompatible with sustainable development. The carrying capacity of natural environments is often exceeded with the addition of tourism demands. Tourist demand for resources (land, water, energy, food) may also compete with the needs of local people and may increase social inequality, gender inequality and injustice. Tourist transport, especially air travel, is highly energy intensive and causes pollutant emissions. Many tourism activities such as skiing, boating, mountain hiking, motorised water-sports (e.g. jet skies), and trekking represent stress for fragile ecosystems. Tourists often lack information and awareness about their impact in a different culture and environment, about their impacts on socio-economic and socio-cultural development, and about the environmental costs of tourism. While tourists may be open to learning, they are often unaware of inappropriate behaviour and have little guidance on how to improve them. Others may refuse to adapt to local life-styles (even when informed) insisting on their freedom to behave as they want.

While the tourism industry may be willing to improve their products and services, there is a conflict between the industry's pursuit of economic gains and social and environmental responsibility. The industry lacks information on the requirements of sustainable tourism and on how to integrate economic forces with environmental and social requirements. Tourists shopping for escapism generally abide by one fundamental consumer ethic: receipt upon payment. Consumer advocates may intervene where inferior customer service is delivered. However, the sustainability of corporate practices is self-regulated. This conflict of interest within the industry, and consumers' low awareness of tourism impacts, have led to a widespread abuse of 'green' labeling.

The mass media, especially television through films and reports about events, sights, etc. in other parts of the world, are increasingly influential on travel decisions and consumer behaviour in the destinations. However, these programmes often serve primarily as advertisements, painting images of destinations, rather than providing relevant information for potential travellers.

There is a lack of reliable and appropriate (e.g. age and gender segregated) research data on the determinants of tourist demand, motivation and behaviour. Few countries, whether tourist-sending or tourist-receiving, collect such data that are helpful under sustainable development criteria. Most studies of tourist behaviour focus on mainstream markets or market segments, rather than assessing or modelling sustainable alternatives. Governments in many tourist destinations and local communities have little or no information on what to expect from tourism and the incoming tourists, and how to influence and control tourism and guide tourist behaviour; They are controlled by international/global institutions, the industry and the consumers. Governments of the affluent countries are only beginning to look at the issues of outgoing tourism. They are not yet sufficiently aware of their responsibility and methods to influence tourist behaviour by political and legal guidelines/criteria and appropriate planning and policies. Trade unions have fought successfully for shorter working hours and more vacation. However, they need to take more responsibility for helping to create a leisure industry that is more sustainable.

Solutions

Consumer behaviour can and must be influenced by:

- Fighting unsustainable forms and aspects of tourism, at the various levels, by sanctioning unacceptable behaviour and discouraging inappropriate consumer behaviour.
- Promoting responsible and sustainable patterns of behaviour, at the various levels, by promoting best practises and encouraging responsible consumer behaviour. There are different types of instruments and remedial measures available:
  - ☐ Legal measures (rules, regulations, sanctions);
  - ☐ Market based instruments, such as taxes to influence market prices;

☐   Promotion of and (financial) support for best practice;

☐   Industry self-monitoring/codes of conduct; and

☐   Information, education and research.

Agents and Partnerships for Changes

Institutional Action and Possible Partnerships

Consumer behaviour in tourism is both a product and cause of policies by government and industry. Therefore, a comprehensive approach is required to solve the problems associated with market-driven tourism. Tourism should be viewed as a major development issue that all stakeholders need to be actively engaged with. To develop effective partnerships, the imbalance of power between the different stakeholders needs to be addressed.

UN Action

- Establish an NGO tourism advisory group for UN to provide technical support, analysis, and strategic advice;

- Create a 'best practices' information clearing-house, in order to collect consumer information useful to understanding and positively influencing consumer behaviour and to make documentation accessible on an equitable basis;

- Initiate a broad information and awareness campaign to highlight damaging forms of tourism and impacts, providing tools for informed decision-making. Initially, target participants in the CSD and CBD processes to clarify roles and responsibilities;

- Research and develop effective certification schemes, form a technical group under the CSD to assess how certification can be improved, e.g. through the review of voluntary codes set up by CSD1998;

- Designate an 'ombuds' office jointly between the CSD, CBD, and UN-CHR to encourage diligent self-

regulation and compliance with international standards
for sustainable tourism; and

- Develop guidance on tourism as an issue within Local
Agenda 21 processes.

Governmental Action

- Introduce and enforce legislation to abolish child
prostitution, implement effective control mechanisms,
conclude judicial assistance agreements;
- Regulate tourist access to ecologically fragile or stressed
natural areas;
- Tourist-sending countries: develop policies on outgoing
tourism from a development perspective;
- Provide frameworks for ecologically appropriate
pricing by strictly applying the polluter-pays-principle
to internalise external costs. This includes ecological tax
reforms including the taxation of aviation gasoline and
oil, removal of subsidies/other economic incentives
with negative environmental impacts.
- Improve conditions for sustainable consumer behaviour
by providing/promoting sustainable tourism facilities;
- Promote environmentally friendly modes of transport
and transport concepts, reduce tourism-related traffic,
shift demand to less environmentally damaging modes
of transport;
- Promote renewable sources of energy (such as solar
power), reduce the use of non-renewable energy and
of limited local resources, through more sustainable
practices/consumption patterns;
- Develop information and education programmes in cooperation with local stakeholders ensuring all
stakeholders' involvement (e.g. women's); provide
information to tourists on appropriate behaviour
(sensitivity, respect for/adaptation to local culture), e.g.
by establishing information centres in destinations, or
by including briefing material for package tours;

- Take into account the specific information needs of various market segments, provide information to the local population on the opportunities and risks from tourism and on how to influence tourist behaviour;

- Adopt, observe, implement and promote codes of conduct, e.g. the planned WTO-OMT 'Global Code of Ethics for Tourism; and

- Integrate sustainable development education including tourism in the curricula of schools at all levels, universities and training institutions, involving all stakeholder groups, create and promote open networks for information and research on sustainable tourism, disseminate and implement results.

Tourism Industry Action

- Promote sustainable tourism products, using market related instruments and incentives, such as contests, awards, certification, model projects, culturally sensitive quality labels covering both environmental and social sustainability;

- Reduce inappropriate consumption, use local resources in preference to imports in a sustainable manner; reduce and recycle waste, ensure safe waste disposal, develop and implement sustainable transport policies and systems, e.g. efficient public transport, walking, cycling in destinations;

- Provide tourists with authentic information, enabling them to understand all environmental and related aspects (e.g. human rights situation) of tourism when selecting any destination or holiday package; educate visitors in advance of arrival and give guidance on 'dos' and 'don'ts'; make tourists aware of their potential impact on and their responsibilities towards host societies;

- Provide information on respecting the cultural and natural heritage of destination areas; employ tour guides who portray societies honestly and dispel stereotypes;
- Ensure that the marketing of 'green' tourism reflects sound environmental policy and practice; use non-exploitative marketing strategies that respect people, communities and environments of destinations, dismantle stereotyping, integrate sustainable tourism principles when creating new marketing strategies;
- Train staff to foster tourist responsibility towards the destinations, encourage multi-cultural education and exchange;
- Actively discourage exploitative sex tourism, particularly sexual exploitation of children, and tourism which causes or contributes to social problems; and
- Adopt, observe, implement and promote codes of conduct.

NGO Action

- Disseminate information to a wide public about the complexity of tourism and about the objectives and criteria of sustainable tourism;
- Educate tourists to change consumption patterns and promote appropriate, environmentally and socially acceptable behaviour in the destinations;
- Launch broad awareness campaigns on the worst impacts of tourism, to be funded by international governmental and non-governmental agencies;
- Promote relevant research on tourism impacts, criteria for sustainable tourism and possibilities for implementation; and
- Monitor tourism development, policy, industry initiatives, and local people's reaction to tourism development and policy, and implementation of stakeholder action.

Promoting Broad-based Sustainable Development through Tourism whilst Safeguarding the Integrity of Local Cultures and Protecting the Environment—Community Development

Problems

Early tourism development has given little consideration to natural resource limitations, impacts on wildlife and indigenous cultures. The human environment and development has been largely ignored. Within the process of globalisation local communities' participation and nature conservation are threatened and often overlooked.

If tourism is to be sustainable, it must improve the lives of local people, protect their environment and health, and offer them a better future. In many instances, tourism can be seen as a vehicle to empower local communities and protect the environment through the development of new employment opportunities, the enhancement of local economies, preservation of indigenous knowledge and practices, public awareness and education. Sustainable tourism can create positive opportunities for community development in remote areas. The business sector can choose sustainable tourism over other more polluting ventures. Long and short-term development plans should be developed so that tourism and its benefits are spread within the area. To develop tourism in a sustainable manner, it is necessary to define optimal tourism destinations in local areas and regions, ensuring enjoyment for the tourist and minimum impact or disruption for the environment and local communities.

Complex and broad-based local communities' involvement in tourism development requires targeted investment strategies implemented by local decision-makers. Those strategies do not exist in many areas and the development of tourism is not planned. Often, tourism investments are imposed from the outside, and the potential for sustainable forms of tourism is weakened. Alternatives to mass tourism (e.g. cultural and "eco-tourism") can be influential in changing the nature of tourism.

Tourism can benefit both tourists and local communities and allow for two-way interaction and education.

Solutions

In order for tourism to become a sustainable industry, countries, states, regions, and individuals must work with new technology, natural resource management and marketing concepts. Ideally, participatory planning and implementation will be a part of Local Agenda 21 processes. To ensure community involvement and to safeguard local cultures, sustainable tourism development should therefore involve all stakeholders in tourism development at all appropriate levels, facilitate the development of tourism services that are planned, managed and reviewed by the host community in Local Agenda 21 processes. This will also ensure that tourism revenue stays in the host communities to enhance livelihoods and generate a profitable source of income, empower and motivate local groups to direct cross-cultural exchange in the way they wish and adopt practices which conserve, protect and preserve the environment.

Local and regional Tourism Boards should be created, involving all stakeholders. These Boards should:

- Promote sustainable tourism concepts in co-operation with local governments and all stakeholders, in line with Local Agenda 21 priorities;
- Work systematically to attract investment in sustainable tourism;
- Help other institutions in developing marketing strategies and training programmes and developing educational materials;
- Work together with different public institutions to involve all stakeholder groups in tourism activities, and bring greater benefits to the entire community; and
- Co-operate with grass-roots organisations to develop employment strategies through sustainable tourism.

Agents and Partnerships for Change

Institutional Action

The UN-CSD should:

- Invite countries to integrate tourism into their sustainable development strategies for the 2002 review;
- Ask the review progress in local communities involvement in tourism development in their country profiles to the preparatory meetings for Earth Summit III in 2002 as part of the review process;
- Instruct DESA in co-operation with relevant UN agencies and convention secretariats, major groups and all stakeholders to develop indicators of sustainable tourism;
- Invite convention secretariats and the Committee on the Environment of the WTO-OMC to report annually to the CSD;
- Establish an international "ombuds" office to deal with human rights abuses and environmental destruction in tourism;.
- Ask UNEP, through their Technology Industry and Economics Division, to work with industry associations at all levels, trade unions, local authorities and NGOs to develop a framework for 'good practice' and to develop a database on good practice, criteria, examples and analysis which should be accessible to governments and stakeholders alike;
- Ask UNEP together with UNCHS, the Sustainable Cities Programme and relevant stakeholders to develop guidance notes on tourism within Local Agenda 21;
- Ask the UN Regional Commissions to prepare a report for the preparatory meetings for Earth Summit III in 2002 on sustainable and community-based tourism activities within their region and to work with UNEP/ WTO to develop regional agreements to address sustainable tourism;

- Invite UNDP to share its work on guidelines for "good practice" and to involve indigenous peoples and local communities this work;
- Ask the UNDP country offices to bring together UN agencies, bilateral donors and other stakeholders to work together on sustainable tourism, as well as involve the gender development programme in this process;
- Ask UNDP to include sustainable tourism into its poverty alleviation strategies and programmes;
- Ask the United Nations Conference on Trade and Development to integrate tourism into their development strategies and include a progress review on the role of indigenous and local communities' involvement in tourism for the Earth Summit III (year 2002) review, and to support community-owned and controlled initiatives in tourism and bio-diversity through its BIOTRADE initiative; and
- Invite environmental conventions and treaties secretariats to include community-based tourism in their action plans and programmes, and to promote it as an incentive for the conservation and sustainable use of bio-diversity.

Multilateral financing and assistance agencies should:

- Provide funds for applied research through pilot projects to determine optimal mechanisms for tourism development in a range of differing circumstances;
- Create small-scale credit lines to assist small enterprises to invest in tourism without excessive risk on personal property;
- Support community controlled tourism initiatives that are directed to poverty alleviation, bio-diversity conservation and promotion of human rights;
- Assess their projects' effectiveness on local, sub-national and national levels involving all stakeholders, and publish the results by the Earth Summit III in 2002; and

- Take part in a discussion forum on minimising leakage, with findings to be brought back to the finance discussion at CSD-8 in 2000. Possible outcomes include the development of a purchasing/procurement strategy for the tourism industry, local/national investment strategies, improved mechanisms for informed choice by consumers, and a linking of aid with capacity building in tourism-dependent areas.

Governments should, at national level

- Establish/clarify institutional and departmental responsibility for developing outgoing tourism and harmonise institutional interventions;
- Initiate the use of tourism for local economic development by involving all sectors alongside the tourist ministry; to build the capacity to work at the destination level, including product development and effective management of existing destinations;
- Facilitate research grants on sustainable tourism, methodologies, impacts and analysis of good practice; finance pilot schemes to develop 'good practice' and establish systems for ongoing evaluation and monitoring;
- Establish sustainable tourism policies and regulations, ensuring responsibly zoned development; natural and cultural heritage and resource conservation and protection;
- Review land ownership in potential tourism areas and where possible transfer ownership to local communities and provide the necessary training for them;
- Include the perspective of local and indigenous communities into local and national sustainable development strategies;
- Increase funding for local NGOs to enable them to engage in a dialogue on tourism;

- Support public education programmes which encourage responsible consumption, natural resource use, environmental protection and local culture conservation;
- Give priority to the following investment suggestions: create funds to help tour operators improve their technical capacity for sustainable tourism development; create funds to develop recreational facilities for the public;
- Encourage local banks and other lending institutions to set up regional investment funding programmes, including micro-credit programmes;
- Create Regional Tourism Boards, fully staffed, to help in planning, promoting, regulating, and expanding sustainable tourism;
- Initiate special marketing programmes by local governments and Tourism Boards, in which local tourism programmes will be advertised in the media;
- Initiate programmes to improve the management of eco-tourism in protected areas; and
- Set up training programmes for guides, tour operators, marketers, etc.

Governments should, at local level

- Harmonise laws on tourism including regulations, fee standards, licensing, etc. so that they will be more favourable to sustainable tourism in the region;
- Ensure that tourism development is in line with Local Agenda 21 priorities and land-use plans and that the public can participate in local and regional decision making;
- Regulate tourism to ensure that profits benefit local people and conservation efforts; and
- Develop and support programmes to revitalise the diverse aspects of local cultures.

The tourism industry should

- Reduce financial leakage and support local economies by buying food and resources locally, develop long-term partnerships with local operators, businesses and suppliers;
- Train and hire local staff and contract with local businesses, promote management opportunities for women;
- Prefer accommodations owned, built and staffed by local people, promote locally made handicrafts and traditional products;
- Encourage clients to study and understand their destinations, respect local cultures and co-ordinate visits with local communities, authorities and women's organisations, being aware of and being sensitive to local customary laws, regulations and traditions, whilst respecting historical heritage and scientific sites; and
- Educate staff to avoid negative environmental and cultural impacts and create incentive schemes to promote sustainable behaviour.

NGOs should:

- Initiate stakeholder dialogue on community involvement in tourism development, recognising social and gender divisions in communities;
- Promote consultation processes in tourism planning, involving local communities;
- Launch educational and awareness programmes on tourism for local communities, support and promote history research and museums;
- Promote the respect for indigenous peoples and local communities' self-determination, autonomy and social and cultural integrity;

- Strengthen their efforts to empower disenfranchised groups (in particular women) to become involved in local tourism planning and management;
- Develop participatory programmes to support the integrity of local cultures and economies;
- Support the sustainable resource use and initiate environmental actions on different levels to conserve the environment while the tourism is developing;
- Analyse the experience with sustainable tourism in different parts of the world, in order to disseminate methodology/positive examples of community involvement in tourism; and
- Support the use of traditional knowledge, practices and innovation systems relevant for the conservation and sustainable use of biological resources and promote actions on different levels to eradicate poverty, protect human rights and conserve the environment while working in tourism.

Possible Partnerships

There is an urgency to constructively shape tourism in order to support local development and conservation goals. UN bodies and institutions, governments, industry and civil society should co-operate to launch a dialogue process on sustainable tourism. This must be planned within the framework provided by the various UN treaties and declarations. All the stakeholders involved in and affected by tourism should be involved in the development of action plans for sustainable tourism. Identifying mechanisms to achieve sustainable development goals in tourism must be a priority for co-operation. 'Good practices' in conserving culture and nature while developing sustainable tourism should be collected worldwide, involving all stakeholders. This process should lead to a multi-stakeholder round-table on strategic planning of local community involvement in tourism to be organised by UNEP as a side event at the Preparatory meetings for Earth Summit III in 2002.

There is an urgent need to assess the impacts of globalisation and the role of multilateral and bilateral development organisations in unsustainable tourism practices. An independent international assessment commission should be created under the CSD. NGOs, indigenous peoples, women's organisations and local communities should be involved in this assessment process together with all other stakeholders. The UN Working Group on Indigenous Peoples should be invited to monitor impacts of tourism on indigenous peoples and local communities. The assessment is to be completed and published by the year 2002.

Coastal Impact of Tourism

Problems

The United Nations Commission on Sustainable Development in 1999 will address both Oceans and Seas and the review of SIDS. Therefore, it is recognising that: "The survival of small island developing States is firmly rooted in their human resources and cultural heritage, which are their most significant assets; those assets are under severe stress and all efforts must be taken to ensure the central position of people in the process of sustainable development." With these words, the Report of the Global Conference on the Sustainable Development of Small Island Developing States identifies the single most important issue to be borne in mind as we address the challenge of survival and development for our islands.

Article 25 of the Programme of Action from the United Nations Conference on the Sustainable Development of Small Island Developing States (SIDS) focuses our attention on another significant consideration: "Sustainable development in small island developing States depends largely on coastal and marine resources, because their small land area means that those States are effectively COASTAL ENTITIES"

Tourism is one of many anthropogenic activities with a special focus on coastal areas. The two most popular locations for holidaymakers are the mountains and the coast. The coastal area or zone (as it is often called) is hard to define as the area where fresh and salt waters mix, containing many complex, diverse and productive ecosystems on and offshore interacting with each other. New concepts including the whole watershed area seem to be the best approach, especially when aquatic pollution problems are considered. Most problems are related to conflicts between different uses and access restrictions. Tourism leads to increased traffic flow and overcrowding in already densely populated areas. Up to 130 tourists has been calculated per inhabitant in the most popular coastal regions. Therefore, tourism adds substantially to the following pressures:

- Pollution by waste water, garbage, heating, noise and traffic emissions;
- Encroachment of buildings, facilities and roads close to the coastline;
- Beach erosion due to building, dune removal and dredging;
- Excessive use of natural areas;
- Destruction of natural areas to accommodate tourism or other needs;
- Inter-sectorial competition and conflict over (marine and terrestrial) space;
- Exclusion of local communities from any role of significance in decision-making;
- The loss of natural and architectural heritage in the face of rapid expansion;
- Strain on public utilities and facilities;
- displacement of local population;
- Creation of restricted exclusive zones that are off-limits to the local people; and
- Loss of business by local enterprises as all-inclusive resorts supplies all the needs of their guests.

Additional typical tourism impacts are socio-economic conflicts as property and general costs of living increases, and social structure can be changed significantly, when summer guests overrun small communities. Foreign customs and expectations can create conflicts and a deterioration of cultural and regional values.

Solutions

A major focus should be on the integration of tourism planning and operation of tourist facilities into local planning instruments. Local agenda 21 can play a key role here in ensuring the involvement of all stakeholders. Ideally, this would be done in the context of integrated coastal area management (ICAM). This instrument bridges sectorial approaches in order to avoid or mitigate user conflicts, and it ideally takes into account ecosystem features and physical, not man-made borders. New tourism developments should be planned together with municipal, industrial, agri-/aqua-cultural and nature protection activities, to allow for multiple complementary uses and to segregate conflicting activities. Area development plans should inform sector plans which should then be incorporated into a coordinated national development plan. All planning should be accompanied by widespread public information dissemination and provide opportunity for discussion leading to integrated coastal zone management. The tourism development strategy should protect local culture, respect local traditions and promote local ownership and management of programs and projects, so as to foster community stewardship of the natural resource base. Environmental Impact Assessment (EIA) on a strategic level as well as for projects is an invaluable tool for this stage. Criteria for planning and EIA should be:

- Strict environmental standards for solid, liquid and gaseous waste emissions;
- Taking the integrity of coastal values and resources into account;
- Enhancement of public transport infrastructure (train, boat, bike, bus);

- Locally adapted styles and maximum height/size limit for facilities;
- Setting of local/regional carrying capacities on a case-by-case basis;
- Limits to sale of property to foreigners;
- Maintenance of public access to the coastal strip; and
- Safeguarding cultural values and customary uses.

During the operation of tourism facilities, several instruments can be applied to enable sustainable development. The details have to be developed according to the use, and together with the local community, the facility operator and local NGOs. Local Agenda 21 could play an important role here (They will be different for a diving site than for a big hotel complex). Modern instruments, which should be, and partly are, already applied in the tourism industry are:

- Introducing environmental management, (according to ISO 14,000 or the European EMAS Initiative);
- Increasing cultural and nature awareness of guests through interactions with local initiatives, guided nature walks, museums, etc.; and
- Integrating the local economy by giving priority to local produce (e.g. fish, fruit, vegetables, furniture, and building materials).

However, all these efforts will be in vain, unless carrying capacity limits can be agreed upon in a dialogue and on a case-by-case basis. These limits have to follow sustainability criteria and have to come out of discussions on the development objectives and the natural and cultural values to be protected. They can be tiered in respect to nature used, number of beds and other facilities for guests, and amount of property to be sold to foreigners. (But management efforts for sustainable development cannot allow an ever increasing growth, which will destroy and, in fact already has, the resources the guests have come to see and experience.) To diminish conflicts a better use of facilities over the year, instead of only in a short season of two to three months should be aimed at. These limits probably have to be stricter for "nature use". Here the introduction and implementation of ranger and guide systems together with limits, regarding the number of visitors, can lead to increased awareness and control at the same time. A simple example is the different approaches to beach litter: Instead of excessive beach cleaning of all organic matter, a plastic litter clean-up by volunteers plus hands-on teaching on the biota originally inhabiting the beach and its natural detritus (like algae and wood) could reinstate an appreciation of nature.

We also believe that the recommendations for action at the national, regional and international levels have been detailed in the SIDS Programme of Action (1994), at the CTO Conference on Eco-tourism in Dominica (1997) and more recently in the CEP Technical Report No. 38 (1997) need to be implemented.

Agents and Partnership for Change

Institutional Actions

Actions on several levels are necessary. First and foremost, the historically grown sectorial approach to managing coastal issues, relating to tourism and other uses, has to be changed substantially. Under the lead of one coastal agency, all stakeholders, especially local people and NGOs, and also sectorial agencies, small and medium enterprises and industry representatives should meet regularly to promote sustainable development of their coastal area. The planning process and the operation of tourism developments should reflect the country's commitment to the guidelines set out in international accords such as Agenda 21 and the SIDS Programme of Action. Depending on the region, this could mean enhancing human resource development including public awareness building and training; institutional strengthening and networking. Lessons learned in one community should be accessible to others. This will start the ICAM process, which is a goal-directed planning and decision-making process. ICAM leads to inter-agency and inter-sectorial collaboration, resulting in operational decision-making with strong public participation and feedback mechanisms. ICAM could mean in practice:

- To start an environmental management initiative through an award scheme;
- To raise an environmental tax from visitors for small projects, e.g. for funding ranger;
- Training or environmental training for tourism staff;
- To start joint actions with local fishermen, farmers, hotels, or other local initiatives; and
- To develop a tourism master plan for the region.

In the long term, a development plan should be devised and discussed thoroughly in order to achieve a common understanding on the objectives and necessary restrictions. As all coastal areas contain particularly sensitive sites, environmental protection has to feature strongly in this planning process, with representatives from government nature protection agencies and NGOs having an equal standing with all other participants. Depending on the nature of the coastline, regional and intergovernmental collaboration may be necessary in addition to local initiatives. For some issues, such as the reduction of pollution and especially "eutrophication", co-operation on a larger regional scale is necessary. Maybe the Baltic Sea States, consisting of very poor and rich states (can serve as example) are co-ordinating their fight against pollution under the Helsinki Convention, funding projects in neighbouring countries according to a list of hot spots. They have just finished the development of a joint Agenda 21 for the development of the Baltic region, including tourism. Generally, national plans should be converted into area development plans, which would provide the local context within which enterprise-level proposals can be evaluated. All these plans should inform and be incorporated into wider regional plans.

As integrated processes take time, tourism umbrella organisations should start with voluntary self-restraint, until locally adapted objectives have been reached. In the north, which bears the brunt of world-wide tourism, a development of quality tourism should be the focus for the future instead of an increase in quantity. The term quality should include ecological and social carrying capacities at the same time as being economically sustainable. In the south, tourism development objectives should be developed according to the local needs. A specially developed Code of Conduct, taking into account inter-area, the Coastal Code of Conduct by EUCC and the Berlin Declaration on Biological Diversity and Sustainable Tourism, could lead the way. Environmental management should become a standard of operation as well as social accountability thus leading to sustainable development.

Possible Partnerships

Additional to those partners mentioned above, there is a major role for environmental and social NGOs to play. The involvement of local initiatives, heritage and nature protection organisations and agencies can lead to a balanced ICAM process in the spirit of the Agenda 21.

Umbrella organisations, such as scuba diving, boating, and yachting associations should develop and promote the application of codes of conduct focussing on environmental and sustainability issues in their respective fields.

The Convention on Biological Diversity contains an ecosystem approach, which is consistent with the ICAM logic. Its experts could sensibly focus on questions of nature use and ecological carrying capacities for sensitive sites in order to obtain harmonised world-wide standards with legal standing.

The instruments and strategies are all already developed, now is the time to utilise and combine them in local dialogue processes.

Chapter 2

Model Tourism Policies: Case Study of Guyana and India

MODEL TOURISM POLICY: A CASE STUDY OF GUYANA

Basic Features of the Sector

Guyana's Current Tourism Product

Tourism takes diverse forms, each with appeal to a particular class of tourist and with its own implications for the country's infrastructure and revenue earnings from tourism. Guyana is ideally placed to take advantage of eco-tourism, which is currently the fastest growing segment of the tourism industry. The potential of eco-tourism today parallels the potential of the "sun, sea and sand" locations in the Caribbean when that tourism market was emerging forty years ago. However, eco-tourism is an entirely different industry and Guyana is uniquely placed to take full advantage of it because of two basic comparative advantages. First, the diversity of Guyana's flora and fauna, the virgin rainforests and the vast array of waterfalls, rivers and creeks are unique factors that set Guyana apart from her Caribbean neighbors who rely heavily on tourism. These are in a virtually pristine state on a scale that is rare in today's world. The second advantage is the fact that Guyana is the only English-speaking country in the South American Amazon Basin. This advantage cannot be underestimated in terms of its appeal to markets such as Europe, the United States and Canada, which are the main markets connected with eco-tourism.

However, eco-tourism development must be pursued in with extreme care and consideration for the natural environment. This is the eco-tourism dilemma, to find a balance between exploiting a natural site for eco-tourism activities without destroying the very location that the activity depends on. Any eco-tourism venture undertaken has to take this into account.

Pertinent Characteristics of Visitor Travel to Guyana

The recently conducted Visitor Survey of Guyana by the Caribbean Tourism Organisation in cooperation with the Guyana Statistical Bureau and the Ministry of Trade, Tourism and Industry provides many insights into the basic features of the sector. The survey shows that the main distinguishing feature of the Guyana visitor profile is a relatively high proportion of business visitors and persons visiting friends and relatives. The peak season for Northern visitors to Guyana is in the winter months. Most other characteristics of visitor traffic reflect these basic facts.

Of the total of 112,751 non-Guyanese who visited in 1994, it is estimated that the overwhelming majority are Guyanese who have acquired other nationality, returning to visit family; business persons; international volunteers and members of NGOs; and visitors on official business. It is estimated that of the arriving foreigners no more than 2,000 come primarily for tourism, as the term is commonly understood. These persons would spend, on average, the equivalent of a few hundred US dollars per stay, certainly less than US $1,000. Therefore, in very approximate terms, it may be calculated that the sector at present generates between 1 and 2 million US dollars per year in foreign exchange earnings. However, the potential would be considerably more than that with a systematic effort to improve the country's infrastructure and develop an appropriate tourism programme.

The Opportunity

Some pertinent facts about tourism that demonstrate its potential impact are:

- The economies of other countries, not unlike Guyana, have been transformed in short order by tourism.
- Travel and tourism are on the brink of becoming the world's largest single industry.
- Even in a highly developed economy like Britain's with industries of vast size, tourism is the second biggest industry.
- Worldwide tourism receipts are projected to grow by anything from 3 per cent to 6 per cent annually for the next ten years; the industry is estimated to be worth over US $3 trillion in 1996.

The overall benefit of tourism is that most of the steps which a developing country needs to take in order to improve its standard of living are exactly those which are required to develop tourism within a country. Some of the benefits of tourism are:

1. A larger tax base for national development.
2. The generation of foreign exchange.
3. The provision of national employment.
4. The promotion of rural and interior development.
5. Human resources development.

Tourism is not simply an attempt to save the environment; it is also an important opportunity for Guyana's economic development. Properly managed, it is a non-depleting, non-consumptive industry that provides ever-increasing economic benefits in a sustainable manner.

Policies of the Sector

There is little evidence to suggest that a tourism policy existed prior to the 1990s, either implicitly or explicitly. Several factors may have been responsible for this. First, the Government may have felt that Guyana does not possess what it takes to be a tourist destination. Second, the apprehension that impacts associated with tourism would exacerbate social problems discouraged the development of tourism. However, in recent years the emergence of eco-tourism as an alternative to resort-based mass tourism has generated an awareness of Guyana's potential for a more beneficial, less intrusive type of activity.

Tourism Policies From 1989 to 1992

In 1989 a study funded by the European Community (EC) formulated a policy framework for the sector. The study recognised the importance of tourism in the generation of employment and the creation of income. A number of recommendations were made, including:

1. The maintenance of effective consultation with all sectors of the tourism industry to create a harmonious relationship between the public and private sectors.
2. The provision of fiscal and other incentives to attract foreign investment and entrepreneurial skills to accelerate new development and to obtain a critical mass in the range of accommodation and attractions.
3. The identification and removal of obstacles and deterrents to new investment and the expansion of existing businesses with tourism potential.
4. The improvement of both internal and international airline connections to foster tourism.
5. The protection of the natural beauty of the country through legislative and other Government measures.

These recommendations were accepted and ratified by the Government, but most have not been translated into practice. Most of the recommendations remain applicable today.

Current Policies

While a written tourism policy does not exist, certain policy decisions have been instituted to give guidance to the tourism industry. These are as follows:

1. Removal of the visa requirement for the major tourist generating markets, in Japan, North America, Western Europe and Scandinavian and Commonwealth countries, as of 1993.

2. The introduction of a 10 per cent room tax on all establishments with a capacity of fifteen (15) or more rooms. However, the funds raised from this tax are not channeled back into the industry.

3. A tourism incentive package that granted duty free concessions to a number of items was prepared for the sector in 1995. Investors have expressed total frustration at the bureaucratic bottlenecks in accessing these concessions. These concessions in their present form do not offer any meaningful incentives to the industry.

4. The Government's decision to commission the Organisation of American States (OAS) to develop an Integrated National Eco-Tourism Development Plan, of which a Management Plan for Kaieteur National Park is a component.

5. The promotion of 1996 as "Visit Guyana Year" with the aim of attracting 250,000 visitors to Guyana; this effort has been perceived by the industry as poorly conceived and premature, with no input from the private sector.

At the same time, Government has strengthened the Tourism Division of the Ministry of Trade, Tourism and Industry. There have been attempts at enhancing the image of the Timehri International Airport and sensitising Immigration and Customs Officers to their new obligations in a tourist destination. Efforts are being made to educate the general population about the new tourism initiatives through the media and other initiatives such as the 1996 Tourism and Environmental Exposition.

Description of Principal Issues and Constraints Facing the Sector

Issues

Clear Definition of Tourism Products in Guyana

Before any real and meaningful development of tourism in Guyana can take place it is necessary to have an understanding of the type of tourism products that are both suited to and suitable for Guyana. Efforts to develop these products and Guyana's image as a destination must be done in accordance with what Guyana determines to be its needs. This requires a precise definition of the types of tourism that are compatible not only with the product that Guyana has to offer, but also with what the country hopes to achieve from tourism development. It is also necessary to examine aspects of tourism which are undesirable for this country.

Forms of Tourism Suited to Guyana's Natural Product and Development Goals

The main tourism markets that are considered to be suitable or potentially suited to Guyana are:

Eco-tourism: Eco-tourism is a natural choice for Guyana for several reasons. First, Guyana's vast and pristine rainforest and savannahs, the abundant wildlife and spectacular natural attractions make Guyana a prime destination for eco-tourists. They are now looking for new, relatively untouched environments, and Guyana stands in a good position to take advantage of this as long as sustainable development techniques are used. Another signal advantage that Guyana has over many of its competitors in the region is that, as mentioned, it is the only English-speaking part of the Amazon Basin.

Eco-tourism is itself advantageous to Guyana because it endeavours to respect the natural environment and different cultures. It is a type of tourism which concentrates on small numbers of tourists paying relatively high prices, thus maximising the economic benefits to the country (which is after all the major reason for tourism development) while minimising the negative effects on the environment and society which are generally associated with traditional or mass tourism. Eco-tourism itself is a very broad classification and ranges from "soft" eco-tourism, which can include luxury accommodations, to "hard" eco-tourism, which focuses more on the surroundings in its natural form and less on personal comfort. To develop eco-tourism, more lodges are needed around the country in key locations, along with better transport and improvements in public health. In particular, it is essential to reduce drastically the incidence of malaria in the interior. A system of national parks and protected areas also needs to be established, preferably around these key attractions.

A basic element of eco-tourism is information and education. Most eco-tourists want to learn more about the environment, both physical and human, that they are visiting. On an international level this requires that adequate information be readily available and accessible to the potential visitor through literature (promotional and information-based) as well as through existing and emerging technologies such as the Internet and CD-ROM. On a local level, the transmission of information necessitates highly trained tourist guides who can communicate and interpret nature in a way that is entertaining and educational. The eco-tourist is typically a well educated, well traveled, professional (generally over 35-40 years old) with a high income and keen environmental, social and political awareness. He or she has probably traveled to several island destinations over the past 10 years and is now tired of the same routine. Eco-tourists are looking for new ways to escape the winter and big city pressures. At the same time, such persons easily see through operations that do not respect the environment or indigenous populations. If Guyana is serious about eco-tourism it needs to embrace overarching environmental policies and ethics, so as not to be perceived as a "fake".

Adventure tourism: Adventure tourism is another growing segment of the tourism sector and can also be divided into "hard" and "soft" categories. It is a sub-sector of eco-tourism. The safety of tourists undertaking this, as indeed all forms of tourism, is of paramount importance since negative publicity or perceptions in this area can have a negative effect on Guyana as a tourism destination in general. It is necessary to ensure that all operators work to high standards of safety and that there is adequate provision for emergency evacuation and medical facilities. The absence of national medical and emergency evacuation facilities is a major hurdle that must be overcome. Tour operators must also be encouraged to have and use appropriate equipment for the various adventure elements of a tour.

Multi-destination tourism: This is a growing segment of the tourism industry, as more and more holiday makers are traveling further distances on vacation and visiting two to more countries. Given Guyana's distance from its main markets of Europe and America and its proximity to the Caribbean, joint destination packages make sense for Guyana, especially in the short term as Guyana builds and expands the products it offers. While eco-tourism is a natural tourism choice in itself for many people, the traditional form of "sun, sea and sand" tourism is still a major attraction for most tourists. Guyana has a unique product which is not widely available in the other Caribbean islands. Good flight connections to Trinidad, Barbados, Grenada and Curacao make these destinations good partners with which to team up to market a joint destination package.

Cruise ship tourism: There is a lot of controversy regarding cruise ship tourism in the Caribbean, and there is a school of thought in Guyana which maintains that cruise ship tourism on a large scale is not compatible with eco-tourism or in the interests of Guyana. This kind of tourism does not increase hotel occupancy rates and therefore much of the tourist expenditure is not spent in the destination country. Potentially large numbers of day tourists can bring detrimental influences to the country, such increases in pollution, crime, drug trade and prostitution. In general, cruise ship tourism requires excellent shopping facilities, including duty free shops, speedy customs and immigration clearance, effective security and short, well co-coordinated tours. This type of tourism can bring revenue into the country in the form of a government head tax and tourist expenditure on craft and other consumer items. However, tourist expenditure is often minimal in comparison to the costs. There is a rough estimate that average revenue obtained by Caribbean countries from cruise ship tourism is about US $5 per head. There is also no head-tax at present on cruise ship tourists to Guyana.

Cruise ship tourism should not be ruled out, but it should be carefully monitored and controlled to ensure that the detrimental effects of mass tourism do not occur. Cruise ship tourists that are here specifically as eco-tourists should be encouraged; there are such cruise ship tourists that visit South America. It is important to note, though, that cruise ship tourism of the wrong kind can destroy the very thing that Guyana is trying to sell.

The business market: A large captive tourism market associated with the business travel already exists. This market can generally be divided into three categories: short-term, long-term and conference travel. The long-term business traveler generally works in or around Georgetown during the week and has the weekend available for travel. The short-term business traveler generally has less time in the country and a less predictable time schedule. However, the country can only handle a small number of business visitors. To cater to large markets, much more infrastructure is needed; service has to be fast and efficient, with all necessary business and communication facilities available.

Heritage/cultural tourism: There is room for the promotion of Guyana's historical sites for their historical and architectural value. Sites suitable for this type of tourism include Georgetown, Fort Island, Magdelenburg and Kyk-Over-Al. Amerindian culture is of potential interest to tourists. However, at the same time it is important to protect these communities from the negative impact which tourism can have on their traditional ways of life.

There are other types of tourism that are possible, such as *industrial* and *agricultural tourism,* which show potential. Tourists have expressed interest in visiting mining and forestry operations and facilities for rum and sugar production. In the case of the first two, these can be tourist attractions only if carried out under strict environmental controls.

While it is hardly likely that many tourists will travel to Guyana specifically to see Georgetown, the beauty of the capital city should not be underestimated in encouraging a tourist in Guyana to stay an extra night. This would have a positive spinoff for restaurants, taxi drivers, craft shops and other local businesses. Measures need to be taken to promote cultural offerings such as art exhibitions and presentations of traditional dance, and to preserve the traditional charm of the city, especially its rich architecture. The spate of concrete buildings being constructed where old Victorian style buildings once existed can only be viewed negatively.

Types of Tourism not Desirable for Guyana

Among the tourism products that are undesirable for development in Guyana are casino gambling and sex tourism, as well as hunting expeditions. Various agencies, such as TAG, have reported an increase in requests for *hunting* recreation but this contradicts the ethos of eco-tourism. The present hunting legislation lays down quotas, lists of protected species and hunting seasons that are questionable. In general, the wildlife trade seriously discredits eco-tourism efforts. In addition, due to Guyana's geography, demographics and human resource constraints, monitoring and enforcement of hunting regulations would be extremely problematic.

Eco-tourism

Because of its importance to Guyana eco-tourism deserves special attention. Eco-tourism cannot be simply classified as nature or adventure tourism. It usually denotes a particular type of tourism that is small in scale and in which local control and local benefits are of primary importance. As it is often closely linked to natural environments and habitats, it necessitates an understanding of the principles of environmental protection and sustainable development. One of the most widely accepted definitions of sustainable development is advanced in the Brundtland Report of 1987 which sees it as development that "meets the needs of the present without compromising the ability of future generations to meet their own needs."

The idea of sustainable tourism is linked to the notions of renewable and non-renewable resources, resource conservation and carrying capacity (*i.e.* the amount of human presence, both long and short term, that specific natural environments and eco-systems can sustain without significant deterioration). It is a dynamic and evolving concept of partnership between humanity and nature and requires the strict management of each resource—land, air, water and wildlife—to ensure optimum value and continuity of supply. There is a convergence between long-term business interests and sustainable development that can be achieved without "cutting corners." At the same time, however, there are a number of socio-cultural, economic and environmental issues that impinge on eco-tourism and on the extent to which it is developed.

It should not be assumed that eco-tourism is a type of tourism in which tourists expect less than other forms of tourism. At the end of the vacation, they expect the same sense of satisfaction and leisure as they would find in other destinations; therefore, eco-tourism has to have fun elements built into it. Visitors must have rewarding and interesting things to do, and it is the responsibility of operators to provide these elements.

Lessons from Other Countries

In planning for eco-tourism, it is useful to learn from the leaders in this new industry, such as Costa Rica and Belize. Costa Rica and Belize have progressed well ahead of Guyana in eco-tourism and "rainforest travelism", and they have some significant advantages over Guyana. In the first place, they both have valuable sea and sand assets; Costa Rica has beaches on both its Atlantic and Pacific sides and Belize has, beside beaches, some of the world's best scuba diving.

Both these countries are closer to the North American markets than Guyana. This not only means cheaper and more frequent flights, but also more primary target cities from which direct flights depart, providing better marketing prospects. Guyana only has direct flight access to Miami, New York and Toronto in North America, and the frequency and quality of air service is well below optimal. Costa Rica (19,000 square miles) and Belize (8,000 square miles), though smaller in size and more advanced in development, also have more accessible interiors with cheaper transportation than Guyana has, with its 83,000 square miles. The consequence of these international and national transportation advantages is that many more potential customers can, conveniently and less expensively, leave home and arrive at a chosen eco-lodge in Costa Rica or Belize without losing an entire precious day of their vacation. It would take two days to get to Guyana from many of their target cities.

In addition to these broad advantages, those two countries have other miscellaneous advantages of varying importance and permanence. They have substantial archeological ruins to visit, active and inactive volcanoes, white water rafting, butterfly farms and well developed nature trails. They are also better able to handle medical emergencies. Costa Rica has long been a preferred retirement country for North Americans, and it has a very positive image compared to Guyana's "Jonestown" reputation. Both countries have established strong and supportive connections with prominent international environmental organisations. Their governments have also invested substantial sums of money into developing and promoting the tourism industry.

One of the most important lessons that can be learnt from the majority of tourism destinations in the Caribbean is the detrimental effects of mass tourism. Islands such as Jamaica, Barbados, and Antigua have regretted their attempts to attract large numbers of discount-rate tourists, who provide a much narrower margin of profitability and add pressure to the local infrastructure. The potential of eco-tourism is closely related to the carrying capacity of the land. Guyana needs to avoid falling into the trap of thinking that the more tourists that visit, the better it is for the industry and the economy. Emphasis should be placed on obtaining the maximum benefits from a minimum number of visitors. Elements of mass tourism that have crept into the industries of Belize and Costa Rica are damaging the very product that they are trying to sell. It is important to note that promotions such as price-cutting have the effect of attracting too many tourists and creating the perception of low quality. Policies therefore need to be adopted that orient the industry away from mass tourism.

Another important lesson to be learned is that the value of a country's offerings increases with time. In a generation or two, the worth of Guyana's natural attractions will multiply several times as such sites become fewer in the world and more people seek relief from choked up developed cities. This has been the experience of Belize and Costa Rica where people are willing to pay increasingly more for the opportunity to visit their attractions. In retrospect, it has also been the experience of Caribbean island destinations; few of these islands would have thought 40-50 years ago that their beaches would be worth what they are today.

Guyana's Advantages

Guyana therefore needs to examine what it has to offer that is special in order to make it a competitive eco-tourism destination. Kaieteur is a terrific asset that should be used intelligently to maximise its value in developing this new industry. With the international language of English spoken by Guyanese, including Amerindians, the country has another major selling point.

But most of all, the singular advantage that Guyana has is that it possesses vast areas of interior that are still pristine compared to Costa Rica and Belize, and most of Panama,

Venezuela and Brazil. Further, Guyana's virtually untouched forests are so diverse that they can show the entire spectrum of tropical rainforest at its best. Where most of Guyana's competitors have comparatively small pockets of rainforest, most of which have farms and rural developments nearby, Guyana has vast rainforests and savannahs with many beautiful waterfalls and very diverse flora and fauna that still are relatively intact. It is vital and intrinsic to the development of tourism to protect the integrity of Guyana's natural environment as a major selling point.

The beauty of the country's ninety miles of Shell Beach and Mangrove Swamp is unique. The four species of sea turtles laying eggs, the bird life, the tropical swamp life, the raw, wild flavor of this coast has to be experienced to be fully appreciated. The expansive southern savannahs are another entirely different tropical ecosystem; there, instead of sea turtles Guyana has unique river turtles. There is bird life such as the Harpy Eagle where the forested mountains meet the savannahs; to a bird enthusiast the Harpy alone provides more reason to visit Guyana than Kaieteur Falls itself. The petroglyphs (some of which are estimated to be over 6,000 years old), are indications of ancient civilisations. The cultural diversity and friendliness of the Guyanese people are also major advantages.

Protected Areas

The establishment of designated protected areas for Guyana is important for distinguishing between those areas to be protected and those to be utilised for extractive industries. Guyana is the only country in South America without a protected areas system. This is a major handicap for a country that is aiming to develop eco-tourism. To correct this situation, the Government has commissioned a team of scientists to prepare a project for a National Protected Areas System (NPAS) in Guyana. The NPAS project is being supported by the Global Environment Facility of the World Bank. Preparatory stages of the project involve collaborative efforts with Conservation International and the Smithsonian Institute. Additional work on protected areas is being conducted through the Amazon Co-operation Treaty (ACT), under which one project examines options for compatible economic development of the Amazon, through possible eco-tourism ventures. From the perspective of protected areas, eco-tourism may symbolise a new and promising way of protecting fragile ecosystems by enhancing their economic value in a sustainable manner.

The Iwokrama Rainforest Programme also offers potential for combining protected areas with tourism and this should be fully explored. The use of 360,000 hectares of virgin rainforest presents an opportunity for the development of eco-tourism and international cooperation based on the principles and practices of sustainable development. In fact, the Iwokrama project has already embarked on an undertaking that would train tourists on various aspects of the forests and surrounding ecosystems. It is expected that future protected areas would also allow for some form of eco-tourism including the education of tourists. Given the high educational element involved in eco-tourism, more international environmental agencies as well as scientific and medical research organisations could be vigorously encouraged to set up operations in protected areas that welcome visitors and study groups. This has been done successfully in many eco-tourism destinations. The Audubon project on Shell Beach is an example of such a combination of environmental research and protection operations, which should be actively sought by the Government as a definitive component of its tourism policy.

Linking tourism to conservation in National Parks requires that the economic gain by investors be coupled with at least two additional goals, benefitting the Amerindians. First, a tourism/conservation programme, as planned for the Kanuku Mountain range or the Kaieteur National park, etc., ideally should extend the economic benefits of development to a broad base of the local human population through employment, compensation fees, or the development of social services. This was the approach taken in Kenya's Amboseli National Park, where it was demonstrated that local people were likely to protect lands and wildlife when they had an economic incentive to do so. The same would apply to the Makushi people who live at the foot of the Kanukus.

Second, tourism in these protected areas should be supported not only by research on the human impact of tourists on the ecosystem, but also by the creation of some mechanism that would allow visitors to contribute to the park following their visit. Excited by their experience, they may want to help, either through direct contributions to a conservation group working in the locality of their visit or though word-of-mouth advertising of the facility.

Private protected areas should also be encouraged. These areas need not be large; there are some in Costa Rica that are just 5,000 acres in size, although the weight of scientific evidence is increasingly in favour of larger areas.

Kaieteur National Park

Since Kaieteur Falls is the main tourist attraction in Guyana, its potential demands that it be given special attention in the development of the tourism industry. There is no doubt that the Kaieteur Falls and the surrounding Kaieteur Park constitute such a compelling attraction on a world scale that they could be Guyana's beachhead into the international tourism market.

Yet, Kaieteur, far from being world renowned, is scarcely known at all beyond a small circle of Guyanese and friends of Guyana, and a combination of circumstances has already put it in danger of being spoiled. Although only a few visitors go there, those few, wandering about at will on very fragile soils and in a fragile environment, are sufficient in present circumstances to pose a threat to the viability of the site and to its unique biosphere. Unregulated mining in the Potaro River watershed and the Kaieteur Gorge also poses a threat to the scenic beauty and ecosystem of the area. Thus, with Kaieteur Guyana has the worst of both worlds; it is not the major tourist destination it should be, yielding the great returns it is capable of but at the same time it is already an endangered site. Monitoring and management to protect it against unregulated visitation and illegal activities such as mining are urgently needed if its integrity as a protected area, and indeed Guyana's integrity as an eco-tourism destination, are to be kept intact.

An escape from this unfortunate situation will be found through well-managed tourism as a means of rationally exploiting and at the same time preserving this great natural resource. Tourist visitation to Kaieteur could increase significantly and entail less damage than is currently being done to the site. The key is the proper design and management of visitation. For example, by having sight-seeing visitors follow prescribed boardwalk trails, and by allowing others with more serious interests in exploring the area to move around only with skilled and licenced guides, many more people could enjoy the Kaieteur experience, and they could enjoy it vastly more, than at present. Managed visitation to Kaieteur would bring in the revenue required for financial sustainability of the site and would generate surpluses for general conservation and development purposes.

Fortunately, Government has commissioned a project funded by the Organisation of American States to develop a master plan for the Kaieteur National Park. When complete, this plan will give details for the layout of the site, guidelines for construction on the site and rules for the limits of acceptable change. This plan would be an integral component of the broader Eco-tourism Development Plan mentioned above.

Amerindian Involvement in Tourism Development

Tourism is an economic imperative for Guyana that is likely to benefit Amerindians if properly pursued. It presents Amerindians with an opportunity to build an indigenous industry which is labour intensive and benefits the local communities.

For a start, English-speaking tourists, who make up the majority of visitors to Guyana, will find it easy to communicate with indigenous peoples in the interior. What could follow from this simple advantage is a best case scenario for the involvement of Guyanese Amerindians in eco-tourism ventures. Guyanese

Amerindians are unsurpassed by any other ethnic group in Guyana when it comes to knowledge of the interior and can be trained to deliver that knowledge in a systematic way to tourists. This will contribute to a high quality experience, resulting in positive word-of-mouth advertising, which should lead to an increase in eco-tourist numbers.

The case of exploitation of wildlife is a good example of how an extractive industry could be turned into a sustainable economic venture for Amerindians. The trade does not earn a lot for the trapper, who gets a fraction of the exporter's profits and generally engages in trapping as a monetary supplement to subsistence practices. Jungle wildlife viewing, in contrast, could involve the same trapper, moving from marketing a consumptive, probably unsustainable activity to a non-consumptive, sustainable use for photo or adventure tours. Amerindian bird trappers could convert to guides if the option were available and if it proved to be a better financial deal for them.

When established, the National Protected Areas System could involve Amerindians in its eco-tourism activities. Amerindians could be trained as park rangers and guides, since they have an unrivaled knowledge of the local terrain and its natural resources. Further, they are more likely to remain in these areas in the long-term than the average coastlander candidate filling such positions.

The impact of such measures on Amerindian communities can be significant because the industry is labour-intensive and can provide jobs for large numbers of unskilled workers. The industry can also stimulate local economies through increased local demands for transportation, lodging, food, materials and nature interpretation. Thus, even a relatively small share of tourism revenues can provide an extremely strong boost to the local economy. New job opportunities would stem the flow from villages to the coast, Brazil and Venezuela. There is great potential income for women and other less mobile Amerindians from the sale of handicraft to tourists, promoted by demonstrations and explanations of the craft processes.

On the other hand, jobs linked to eco-tourism could be seasonal and subject to world economic conditions. While eco-tourism is meant to be small in scale, it has the potential to make local communities too dependent upon it. These communities are likely to suffer much more from a decline in the tourism sector than the country as a whole would. For small communities that depend upon agriculture and other primary activities, eco-tourism has the potential to draw labour out of those sectors. For example, in indigenous communities, the craft industry may thrive at the expense of food production.

The influence of foreign cultures may also impact upon communities in such a way that many traditional values may be lost. Some theorists feel that commercialisation of culture can lead to pseudo-culture, folklore specially devised for tourists, alteration of traditional crafts due to commercial pressures, and the replacement of traditional handicrafts by cheap souvenirs.

Before tourism can benefit Amerindians, therefore, there must be fundamental institutional strengthening. This requires a participatory approach that must be applied through direct discussion, education and practical training programmes. Amerindian groups should be empowered to start their own tourist ventures in a small and manageable way. These can grow as experience is gained.

Marketing

Guyana starts off as a difficult sell in the world of tourism. While it has no image in the world travel market, it also has to cope with the negative image of Jonestown and the perception of being a poor, fragile democracy. Compare this reputation to that of a West Indian island like Jamaica, with a history of greater political turmoil and violence, gun-crime and drugs; yet Jamaica, "where the nights are gay and the sun shines daily on the mountain top," benefits from helpful romantic images in the international market place. Guyana is even sometimes confused in name with Ghana in Africa, so one has to be sure that visitors do not get on the wrong plane, going to the wrong continent. Top priorities will have to be filling the gap in knowledge that exists in the world about Guyana and working to erase the current negative images.

Tourism is an export product, but unlike other exports of Guyana, tourism is intangible. To sell tourism is to sell a dream or fantasy, and such a product cannot be weighed or put into a box. The customer buying the tourism product cannot sample it before buying, nor can he or she take it home after purchase. Tourism is a singular and highly personal experience that is slightly different for every visitor. Factors that contribute to a sense of satisfaction with a tourism experience are many, but chief among them are physical beauty (the environment wildlife, etc.), cultural experiences (authenticity of life, historical locations, etc), and a friendly, helpful population.

In marketing tourism it is also important to examine what the overseas market wants. At present, visitors to Guyana can be grouped into the following categories:

- Business people and official visitors with a few days to spare;
- Expatriate Guyanese returning on holiday or business;
- Expatriate workers based in Guyana;
- Tourists coming over for a few days as part of a multi-destination holiday; and
- Tourists coming currently to Guyana for eco-tourism holidays.

The first two categories plus international volunteers currently make up the vast majority of all visitors to Guyana, in fact over 95 per cent of the total number. The total number of visitors to Guyana, a little more than 100,000 annually, is small compared to other tourist destinations, but the potential for growth and resulting foreign exchange is large. Guyana could market itself as part of multi-destination packages, but this requires cooperation with operators from other countries and detailed planning, especially in the coordination of flights, so it may be best left to a later stage in the sector's development.

Guyana needs to realize that marketing is a business and cannot be accomplished though embassies, a past common error among those trying to promote emerging tourism. A visitor looking for a tourist destination spot will not visit every nearby embassy or consulate and, in any case, Guyana does not have embassies and consulates in all of the major target cities. Professional representation in the markets that Guyana wishes to attract is vital. In marketing Guyana's tourism product, planners have to be prepared to spend money. Successful marketing is done through advertising and being sure that Guyana is listed in all travel guides and books. Government also needs to appreciate that tourism is an export industry and should therefore be eligible for benefits normally afforded to other export sectors.

Expansion and Improvement of the Product Offered

A sudden shortage of fuel for internal aviation, which still occurs, means that a visitor's planned itinerary is ruined. Unregulated or badly managed access to prime sites like Kaieteur—or a failure to stop environmental degradation arising from mining in the wrong places—will destroy the assets on which the growth of tourism depends. Inadequately or inappropriately developed lodging facilities and attractions will send visitors home disappointed, never to recommend Guyana to their friends. Insufficient attention to the total quality of the experience that the market wants, from the moment of arrival to the moment of departure, will spoil the potential of Guyana.

It is obvious that there are a number of aspects of tourism that must be in place at the same time to make a successful industry. A failure of any one of the various requirements for the industry will mean the failure of the entire industry. If Guyana is going to be serious about tourism, then all aspects must be working properly at the same time.

Product improvement should be centered on the following areas:

- *General information*: At present it is extremely difficult for the would-be visitor to Guyana to find any reasonable country information in existing literature and guide books. There is a total lack of generic advertising of the country.

- *Easier access to Guyana and its interior*: There are only a few airlines that serve Guyana and these only go to limited destinations. For example, in North America direct flights can only be made to Miami, New York and Toronto. In Europe, only London, Frankfurt, Zurich and Amsterdam are served through Trinidad or Barbados. Attention needs to be paid to upgrading facilities at Timehri so as to attract American and European airlines. The process for obtaining flight rights should be streamlined, so that the industry could work more with airlines to develop new markets.

  The current Guyana Airways Corporation (GAC) service to the interior is totally inadequate to satisfy the needs of Guyanese, let alone tourism. For example, many tour operators report being unable to obtain seats on GAC flights to Lethem, even though TAG holds six seats up to eleven days before flights. The number of locations served by GAC and the frequency of flights are not adequate for the development of the industry. And yet Government regulations restrict the number of commercial seats available on domestic flights. Coordinated efforts between private operators and GAC are required to ameliorate these problems, as well as a change in the regulatory framework.

  Because of the limited road infrastructure the only access to many of Guyana's remote areas suitable for tourism is via light aircraft. There is a shortage of such aircraft to meet the current and future needs of tourism in Guyana. In addition the costs associated with this kind of transportation are high and add to the overall price of Guyana's tourist product. The current high taxes that the private sector pays on aviation fuel, spare parts and aircraft (from which GAC is exempted) add to the cost of this type of transport. There is no level playing field between private airline operations and the Government-owned GAC. There is insufficient free competition in the market to properly develop the airline industry locally. This makes tourism in Guyana uncompetitive with other destinations with better infrastructure and better access to main tourism sites.

- *Improved Infrastructure*: Of all the productive sectors of the economy, tourism is the one that depends most on the physical environment and other ambient conditions that exist in the country. Infrastructure such airport facilities, roads, water systems and medical facilities have to be improved to attract tourists. Tourists often wish to know that when they return from an exotic interior destination they will be comforted by the luxuries of a quality hotel in Georgetown. The importance of hot showers, quality restaurants, smooth roads and courteous airport officials, for example, cannot be underestimated even to the most intrepid backpacking adventure tourist.

- *Reliable medical and evacuation services*: The nature of Guyana's industry is that tourists travel to remote areas often under arduous and sometimes risky conditions. Inevitably there will be accidents and the need for emergency evacuation. At present this recourse is not available, nor are medical treatment and facilities to the level that most tourists would consider adequate.

- *Professional product*: Guyana's tourism product needs to be handled more professionally. This can be achieved through a number of changes such as regulation and monitoring and developing provisions for prosecuting those who fail to comply with the regulations and standards. It also requires further investment at both the private and public levels, especially in providing qualified and skilled staff and fostering a professional atmosphere that encourages a strong sense of commitment, pride and responsibility.

- *Security*: Georgetown in particular has a bad name internationally as a dangerous city. In reality, it is probably safer than many cities around the world, but Guyanese over-emphasise the problem instead of taking corrective measures. Extra police and lighting are needed in principal tourist locations in the city and on frequently-used walkways. Security needs to be increased in key tourism sites; the potential for illegal immigration and the movement of drugs and other restricted goods demands a tighter net of security in these places.

- *Streamlining the procedure for obtaining interior permits and visas*: An interior permitting procedure is standard policy to ensure that Amerindians are protected. However, the system should be streamlined so that applications to travel to the interior can be processed quickly. Tourists only have limited holiday time and will not tolerate sitting in a government office for hours; they will simply leave and visit a more organised country. To properly regulate visitation to the interior, permits should only be granted to tourism companies who have a proven track record and are willing to respect the communities they are working in.

- *Public liability insurance*: International wholesalers and operators often inquire as to whether local operators carry public liability insurance. This requirement often determines whether an international operator will sell the Guyanese tourist product. Most local operators would like to carry such insurance but it is either unavailable or too expensive. This is an important area of concern as the nature of Guyana's product means that there will always be a risk of accidents. In the absence of insurance, the operators themselves are subject to payment of claims made by tourists, in amounts which can severely damage a small scale operation. Furthermore, the amount of compensation that would be awarded by a Guyanese court would not be international y comparable. The repercussions for Guyana in such a case would be severe and wide-reaching due to the adverse international publicity and the fact that the country as a whole can be blacklisted as a high risk destination.

Standards Within the Industry

There is a strong feeling of responsibility among operators to maintain a good reputation for the industry in Guyana as a whole. This means a degree of self-regulation could work beneficially to prevent rogue operators from damaging the reputation of everyone, especially when the industry is in such an early stage of development. The Tourism Association of Guyana can play a role in assisting a national regulatory agency to monitor the industry and indeed it is currently developing standards for safety. There are also plans to develop guidelines to cover other aspects of quality control in the future. The Association cannot by itself function as a regulatory body; it can provide checks and send warning signals to relevant authorities, and it can help educate operators, but enforceable legislation and regulations are needed.

Areas in which standards and regulations are urgently needed include:

- Standards for licensing tour operators.
- Regulations for building eco-tourism resorts.
- Standards for other customer servers such as taxi drivers, boats, hotels, restaurants, employment of staff, etc.
- Land use.

The enforcement of these standards will be vital for a successful industry. The standards must be accompanied with stiff penalties that are compatible with the severity of the infringement.

Investment

First and foremost, it must be remembered that eco-tourism is a business. Investors and bankers will only support the industry if the profit potential justifies the high financial risk. The key to its success is achieving high occupancy rates and filling tours. Policies that protect the environment and promote safety, and the like, are irrelevant in the absence of policies that could attract investment.

The Guyanese tourism industry is currently considered to be a high risk business by investors and bankers. The country is simply not perceived as a good investment in tourism because of the multiple risks involved. In addition to the financial risks normally associated with tourism itself, there are problems peculiar to Guyana related to the fact that the country's democracy is still in a stage of consolidation, to the uncertain overall investment climate and to the fact that Guyana is hardly known and that eco-tourism is still an emerging market. Investors are very skeptical: all things considered, the potential return often does not instill confidence, and investors would prefer to take their tourism investments elsewhere.

Relevant points for consideration when formulating investment policies for tourism are:

- Guyana has no track record with respect to tourism.
- Eco-tourism is itself still an infant industry.
- After opening a resort or a tour operation, it takes between eighteen months to two years of extensive marketing efforts before customers of any significant numbers can be attracted.
- Contingencies have to be built into each plan, providing for periods of low occupancy rates, delays before a profitable level of business is achieved, natural disasters, etc.
- The investor has to periodically spend money bringing the press, tour operators, Caribbean owners or managers (for joint tours), interested travel agents, and

to prepare brochures, video tapes, etc. These costs are considerably higher during the start-up period.

- Lodges and tours for eco-tourism are generally small. Thus there are high per capita overhead expenses.

- Because of the high risk involved, investors need higher returns to satisfy the bankers' payback period of 5 to 6 years.

- Twenty-five per cent of the gross selling price of a resort room has to be paid to the tour operator and be used to service bank charges such as the use of American Express, etc. Another 10 per cent has to be devoted to cover advertising costs. The resort then has to cover operational expenses and make a profit with the remaining 65 per cent.

- Bankers would like to know that they can recover and transfer all property and land of an eco-tourism resort, as an adequate means of collateral in the event of a failed operation.

At the same time, capital investment in eco-tourism in Guyana is between a quarter to a third of the per unit cost of a similar investment in the Caribbean. The typical capital investment cost per unit at an eco-lodge is about US $35,000 with appropriate fiscal concessions and infrastructure already in place (*i.e.*, roads, air strip, etc.). A similar unit in a Caribbean destination is about US $100,000. Bankers may be willing to back such investments, provided the concerns mentioned above are mitigated.

Education and Public Awareness

The behaviour of eco-tourists can be an important issue. One does not become environmentally sensitive and responsible simply by booking onto an "eco-tourism" holiday or day trip. Tourists should not only be educated about their responsibilities to the environment, they should also be educated about the environment. In fact, the latter is a major component of an "eco-tourism" vacation whereby visitors have an opportunity to put their cameras down and engage in dialogue with their hosts. It is useful for native people in a host country or region to recognise the elements of the natural environment that may be new and of interest to the visitor. Natives guides in particular should be alert for the "teachable moment" that creates a bond between host and visitor. A true eco-tourist is also an "anthropotourist", deriving pleasure and satisfaction from learning how the environment is viewed through the eyes of local people.

Local people also need to be educated to the potential impacts of receiving tourists as well as the expectations of such visitors. While it is certainly most important for local peoples to take pride in their customs and culture, it is also important to have an understanding of the travelers and their perspective on activities that may give rise to what is termed as "culture shock."

There are also misguided perceptions about tourism among the wider Guyanese public that need to be dispelled such as:

- That Guyana lacks true beauty and has limited tourism potential. (On the contrary, the tourism product is not limited, rather it is specialised.)
- That applying the traditional image of tourism, largely based on the Caribbean model of sand, sea, and sun is the only valid one.
- That the tourism industry benefits only a few.
- That the industry is one of servitude. (Rather, there is an important difference between servitude and professional service.)

An informed and trained citizenry is the backbone of any successful development process; education is the key. Guyanese need to appreciate the great value that the interior represents to the peoples of the densely populated urban cities of the developed world. A community that understands tourism is one that would be better able to benefit from it. Its development demands that the industry be developed and fashioned in the best interest of both the visitor and the residents of the community. This can only be done by creating an appropriate attitudinal environment and educating persons within the local community to talk about tourism as a viable alternative in Guyana. This should eventually lead to a wider understanding to the benefits of tourism and the roles of society in this new industry.

NGOs can be a valuable source of funding and training of guides and other tourism-related staff. The Tourism Studies Unit at the University of Guyana could be strengthened to play an important role in educating the general public and disseminating accurate information. It can work in coordination with the Government's tourism regulating body, TAG and other NGOs, as well as the Carnegie School of Home Economics, hotels, and other tourism agencies. It should, however, guard against teaching a generic tourism product as opposed to teaching about the uniqueness of Guyana. Thus it should incorporate practical, on-the-job experience in its programme.

Partnerships in the Industry

The Tourism Division: At present, Government regulation and support services for the tourism industry are provided through the Tourism Division in the Ministry of Trade, Tourism and Industry. This division was created in July, 1991, and emerged out of a reorganisation of the Public Service in 1990. Its creation hinged on a policy decision to formally establish a tourism industry in Guyana. One of its major functions is to co-ordinate the activities of the industry.

This division is also responsible for:

- The execution of national policy related to tourism.
- The formulation and monitoring of tourism guidelines and regulations.
- The marketing of the country's tourism image.
- Human resource development for the industry.

The Tourism Division is also a member of the Caribbean Tourism Organisation (CTO) and functions as the local coordinating agency for CTO activities. Much effort in the Division has also focused on international marketing and development of the product and the required human resources.

Despite its best efforts, the Division of Tourism is understaffed and lacks the internal systems and structures for the smooth facilitation of programmes and activities required for its work. It is affected by many of the same ailments that are prevalent in other Government departments, such as a shortage of skills, a lack of facilities and no legal mandate to perform many of the functions that are required of the department.

The Tourism Association of Guyana Limited (TAG): The Tourism Association of Guyana represents its members' interests in a number of ways by providing them with advice and assistance on marketing their products and making available all information concerning the promotion of Guyana abroad. It also deals with enquiries about tourism and passes on information to its members and to interested parties abroad. The Association has tried to promote the interests of its members by ensuring that high standards of safety and product quality are maintained throughout the industry. Plans are underway to certify all members meeting the required levels of safety and standards required by TAG but this cannot, and should not, replace government regulation of the industry, as TAG cannot by its very nature function as a national regulatory body.

There have been questions about TAG's membership and how well it represents all the interests associated with Tourism. The list of potential members is quite long since tourism impacts on all sectors of the economy and the increase in tourist arrivals will ultimately benefit all business in Guyana.

Constraints

There are significant and serious obstacles to the development of eco-tourism. If incorrect perceptions and misunderstandings about the sector prevail, then the opportunity for the development of a sustainable industry will be lost. The principal constraints to the development of the industry can be summarised as follows:

Institutional Framework

There is a lack of the required institutional framework to effectively implement, develop, and sustain the eco-tourism industry. This framework involves laws and behaviour codes for both eco-tourism operators and eco-tourists as well as for monitoring activities.

Investment

There is a lack of investment guidelines for an industry in which all investment would have to come from the private sector. This has led to a reluctance on the part of investors to enter the industry.

The problems of investment are also related to the airline industry. The impediments to the development of the private aircraft industry, such as the substandard state of navigational facilities, lack of incentives for investment, regulations that create unequal competition (especially with regard to GAC), the reluctance of international airlines to come to Guyana, and policies that discriminate against new airline operations, among others, directly affect the tourism sector.

Other impediments to investment include high duties and consumption taxes, high interest rates and the generally high cost of doing business in Guyana because of the bureaucratic delays.

Land Use

There is a lack of mechanisms to coordinate the allocation of land to various users, which has led to land conflicts which hamper the desired image of eco-tourism. For example, in areas of potential tourist value, there may be unchecked mining and unsustainable forestry practices. Together with a questionable record on the part of Guyana on protecting and preserving its environment, this takes away from the "green" image that is necessary for the development of tourism.

There is also a lack of adequate land monitoring and regulating mechanisms. Few land use laws are realistically enforceable due to this lack of monitoring and regulating systems.

Quality and Variety of Product

Guyana's tourism product is not yet developed to the extent that it can competitively attract the typical eco-tourist, *i.e.* there are not enough lodges, tour sites, trained guides, etc. The sector currently runs the danger of disappointing visitors.

Infrastructure

There is a general lack of infrastructure to support the tourism industry. This is especially related to airstrip facilities in the interior such as refueling nodes. The absence of medical evacuation facilities is also a deterrent to the development of the industry, as is the prevalence of malaria and deficiencies of the potable water systems.

National Parks

The lack of a national parks system with a framework for managing them does not help to create an appropriate image for Guyana.

Objectives

The broad objective for a tourism strategy policy for Guyana is as follows:

The further development of a tourism industry that balances the economic, social and environmental needs of Guyana to create a sustainable and profitable dynamic tourism sector.

Achieving this sectoral objective will contribute to the national objectives of rapid economic growth and poverty alleviation, the latter because of employment creation effects, especially among hinterland populations.

To achieve this sectoral objective, a number of sub-objectives can be defined as follows:

1. The promotion of an industry that makes appropriate use of what Guyana has to offer and takes full advantage of market trends in the tourism industry.
2. The development of the industry by placing the protection of its natural resource base as its highest priority through the use of sustainable practices.
3. The setting of standards and practices that are commensurate with the market that is being targeted.
4. The development of an industry which ensures that its operations benefit widely the people of Guyana, in particular the Amerindian community.

Policy Recommendations and their Technical Justifications

The central thrust of these new policies for tourism is a focused and unambiguous strategy of pursuing high quality, up-market eco-tourism in controlled numbers that do not exceed scientifically determined carrying capacities of interior sites. All other policies should follow from this central thrust.

Ministerial Responsibility

The Minister responsible for tourism should be the same Minister responsible for the Environment, Protected Areas and Amerindian Affairs in a separate Ministry. This restructuring is fundamental and would result in a single person being able to speak for interests that have a lot in common.

Need for a National Tourism Board

The idea for a National Tourism Board has been tabled for some time. It is absolutely vital that the creation this Board be undertaken urgently. Such a Board would replace the Tourism

Advisory Board and absorb most of the functions of the Tourism Division of the Ministry of Trade, Tourism and Industry. Its main responsibilities would be regulation, marketing, research and product development. This Board should be a semi-autonomous agency with the authority to hire, fire, set salary levels, etc. Funding should be supplied by Government with supplementary funding from licence fees on the industry and a diversion of the hotel room tax. This investment by Government would benefit the country several times over in a short period of time through increased corporate and income taxes, the generation of employment, foreign exchange inflows and through the spin-off effects on other industries.

The composition of the Board is critical for its success. The Board should be composed of no more than nine persons, with five representatives from TAG and four from the Government. This would result in a Board that is widely representative but not too large to manage the affairs of the industry. The Government should have the authority to pick the chairperson from among the nine members. The President of TAG should be an automatic choice as one of the five private sector representatives. Appointments to the Board should be staggered so as to avoid the arbitrary replacement of members when the Executive of TAG or the Government changes hands.

It will be the Board's responsibility to overesee the implementatioin of many of the recommendations stated in this chapter.

The Role of the Tourism Association of Guyana

Currently, the Association is made up mostly of tour operators, resort owners and hoteliers, but it is being widened to include representatives from all sectors of the economy that have an impact on, or can benefit from, tourism. Consideration is already being given to including the mining and forestry private sector groups as associate members, and efforts are continuously being made to invite Amerindian representatives to join TAG.

The Association will continue to set minimum standards with which all members serving the industry must comply. Certification will be given only to those who meet or exceed these standards. The Association should develop classification and grading schemes for its members that can be based on physically measurable criteria. For example, in the case of tour operators, it can be based on the number of passengers the operator puts into a boat, the type of aircraft that is used, or the provision of education on the ecosystem etc. These classifications can make tourists aware that Guyana is serious about tourism and as the sector in Guyana grows it can assist international certifiers in grading Guyana's product. Standards set by TAG will not supersede those set by the Tourism Board.

Protected Areas

A large percentage of tourists can be expected to visit National Parks. Parks therefore need to be carefully regulated, and the lines of responsibility for these parks must be clearly delineated. For example, responsibility for protected areas should be removed from the Ministry of Health and placed in the hands of appropriate authorities, through the reorganisation indicated in subsection A above.

It is important that certain criteria be established for each protected area in the interest of tourism. Among these are definitions for the carrying capacity of each and guidelines for visitation. Among the guidelines for visitation will be specifications regarding the length of stay, requirements for trained guides, means of access, controls on the removal of flora and fauna and the taking of pictures, visitation by individuals or groups, etc. Within the park itself there may be areas in which absolutely no one is allowed to go, for protection of the area's biodiversity.

The boundaries of the Kaieteur National Park should be determined as a matter of urgency and all mining in the Kaieteur watershed and the gorge below the falls should be immediately stopped. Among the major tasks that must be accomplished as a matter of priority are to:

- Obtain a definitive boundary survey and posting the perimeter.
- Obtain a topographic survey with the appropriate contour intervals identified for a more detailed study.
- Develop consultative mechanisms for incorporating representatives of local Amerindian groups in the decision making concerning the site.
- Locate significant site features, *e.g.*, trees, marshes, streams, existing structures (if any), archaeologically significant areas, etc.
- Obtain aerial photographs of the site to confirm survey information.
- Identify a sustainable power source on the site.
- Investigate soil conditions and bearing capacities for the number of tourists and any construction.
- Review the local watershed layout relative to the site, noting activities on adjacent property which may impact on drainage and water quality.
- Investigate present and planned uses for adjacent property.
- Study any significant archaeological sites on the property.

The OAS project for the Kaieteur National Park should be opened for private sector comment before its finalisation and implementation.

International organisations such as the World Wildlife Fund and Conservation International must be invited by Government to conduct additional scientific and other environmental studies in parks, along the lines of the ones that they are currently doing. The support and stamp of approval of these groups is important. These organisations should also be able to attract funds for the parks' maintenance and upkeep. In any case, realistic charges will have to be paid by tourists to enter the parks so as to provide sufficient revenues to cover all costs.

Lessors of large tracts of private land in the interior could also be encouraged to convert these into protected areas. In allocating land among sectors, priority should be given to eco-tourism for the simple reason that the land can be used afterwards for other extractive industries if the tourism venture proves not to be in the best interest of the country. Land that is used for extractive industries cannot be used for other purposes afterwards.

After the initiation of the Guyana Rainforest Foundation linkages should be explored between its activities and programmes to support eco-tourism.

Amerindian Involvement in Tourism

In developing the tourism industry efforts must be made to ensure that Amerindians are involved. Tourism should be started at a slow and measured pace in Amerindian communities so as not to overwhelm local capacity and result in a sudden increase in social stresses. Aiming at once for state-of-the-art tourist lodges may not be the way to initiate eco-tourism ventures in Amerindian communities. There will of course be the need for good business management such as rigorous bookkeeping and accountability for funds received and the reliable supplies of goods and services for guests.

Due to the limited experience that Amerindians have with development projects, tourism ventures to be started and managed by Amerindians will have to be accompanied by:

- A local group with the initiative and willingness to maintain the level of effort that an eco-tourist venture entails.
- Intensive and extensive training of Amerindians in business management, account-keeping, accountability, etc.
- Start-up capital that is affordable and accessible to Amerindians.

- A commitment by central Government and funding agencies to work to sustain Amerindian ventures in the eco-tourist field.
- The encouragement of partnerships between Amerindians, investors and nature and conservation NGOs in developing tourism sites.
- Continuous information-sharing and consultation with Amerindians in the development of tourism.

Clearly, all of these requirements cannot be fulfilled by Government or the tourism industry only. Non-governmental organisations and others will have to play a role. Other aspects of the National Development Strategy with respect to Amerindian affairs have to be incorporated. For example, given Government's fiscal constraints, it is unlikely that it can be depended on to provide subsidised loans. However, the establishment of an Amerindian Development Fund will provide a source funding. National Development Strategy, Amerindian Policies, provides more details on the proposed Fund. The use of such funds for tourism ventures presents an ideal opportunity for the sustainable development of Amerindians.

Amerindian involvement may also provide the more affordable alternative that Guyanese need in order to visit the interior. This could have the spin-off effect of allowing other Guyanese to observe Amerindians in their interior environment and utilise their services as guides, teachers, etc., which would lead to a greater respect for the indigenous community.

With regard to tour operators entering Amerindian communities, guidelines need to be established for gaining permits. An overall code of conduct should be developed between tour operators and the Amerindians that all tourists must follow. Such a code should provide guidelines for taking photographs, access to sacred sites, times of visiting, etc. It will be the responsibility of tour operators to educate tourists about these regulations before visiting Amerindian communities. Failure to do so could result in licences being revoked.

Individual Amerindian communities may develop stricter codes. The collection of head fees by Amerindian communities should be legislated.

Finally, of course, Amerindians will decide for themselves if eco-tourism ventures are worth the trouble or not. They would also have to find ways to limit or mitigate the stresses of this new industry. In each case, the community in question should decide on the soundness of eco-tourism on a project-by-project basis.

Investment

Tax Concessions and Exemptions

Since tourism is essentially a private sector enterprise, the right conditions to attract private investment must be in place. Investors must feel a sense of security about investing in a country and a sector that are perceived as high risk. By international standards of the industry, the first concession would be a tax holiday on all capital investments in the sector for five to seven years. This is below the ten-year concession that is commonly given to developers in Caribbean destinations. Secondly, until the more uniform tax code is implemented, the industry should be given a waiver on duty and consumption taxes for the import of items necessary for the tourism industry. At present, in the absence of these concessions, the industry is stagnant and does not contribute as much as it could to the Government coffers. The returns from granting these concessions would be perceived soon afterwards, basically in the form of higher income tax revenues.

The Development of Lodges

As a practical measure, the Lands and Surveys Department must first of all embark on a special project to eliminate the existing backlog of all applications for land and institute mechanisms for the fast processing of land applications.

The development of lodges can be expected to occur on lands in two categories. The first category includes the obvious areas: next to or in proposed National Parks such as Kaieteur, in the Kanuku mountains, at Shell Beach, or around Orinduik Falls, for example. In the second category would be lands identified by investors at their own expense. Under current land policies, annual lease rates for all lands should be based on a percentage of the gross revenues, say between 2 to 3 per cent, or based on market lease rates, which ever is higher.

In the first category, there can be expected to be more potential investors than can be allowed, especially at places such as Kaieteur top. Therefore, mechanisms need to be put in place for selecting those who will be allowed to build a lodge there. As a first step, there must be minimum criteria set for these location, such as the maximum number of units per lodge. This would ensure that several investors are allowed to invest; thus if it is determined that the area can support only 40 units, then Government may stipulate 5 lodges at 8 units per lodge. The minimum capital investment should also be specified. The locations will then be put up for auction to those who meet the minimum requirements. The bids will be judged on two criteria: the percentage of gross revenues that an investor is willing to pay to Government as annual rent for the land and the capital investment that is proposed for the site over a given period, such as five years. The winning bid will be the one with the highest product from the percentage of gross revenues and the capital investment. This would guard against the possibility of an investor losing the bid when the lease rate offered is smaller than another but the proposed investment is higher.

A portion of the lease rates should be turned over to nearby Amerindian communities. This is an innovative approach because it places the Government, the investor and the Amerindians on the same side of the equation; they would all like to see greater returns to the investment because they all have more to gain. At the same time, the Amerindians have an incentive to protect the land because in the long-term it will represent a continuous source of income. Amerindians can also monitor the operations of the investors with respect to reporting requirements, such as the number of tourists that visit.

In the second category of land, in which an investor identified the land needed for setting up a lodge, the investor must again meet certain minimum requirements before being granted a lease or freehold title to the land. Rights to the land should be given on a first come, first served basis provided the minimum requirements are met. In this case, the lease should be offered at market rates or as a fixed percentage of the gross revenues whichever is higher. The latter arrangement would, however, require careful monitoring because investors might tend to under-report visitation. Again, arrangements could be entered into whereby a portion of the lease payments is diverted for the benefit of nearby Amerindian communities.

In all cases, leases should be for 99 years, be freely transferrable from one person to another and be available for use as collateral. Banks should have the authority to reposess land and property on which an eco-tourism site is built. Whenever possible, lands should be sold to investors in freehold.

Guidelines should also be developed to mandate buffer zones around lodges, the distance between lodges, etc. There should also be certain allocations allowed for Guyanese investors, especially at places such as Kaieteur.

The Government should embark on a project to list all the sites in the interior that have been identified as desirable areas for the development of lodges. Tourism site investment listings have been highly successful in a number of countries in encouraging the right type of investment suitable to the peculiarities and carrying capacity of the land identified.

Financial Monitoring

The new Tourism Board should insist that assessments and reports, financial and otherwise, be prepared by lodge owners in a consistent and timely manner. Bank reports should be copied to the Ministry responsible for Tourism. Severe penalties should be issued for fraudulent reporting and/or non-compliance. Computer-assisted accounting and reporting will help make the process easier and more efficient.

Air Transport

This sector needs to be opened up as soon as possible for effective functioning and to benefit all sectors of the Guyanese economy. With respect to tourism this necessitates the participation of private capital and management in the domestic operations of GAC. This should be accompanied by the freeing up of restrictions on general aviation to allow for more competition. Aircraft owners should also be allowed to decide what type of aircrafts they would like to buy. The management of Ogle aerodrome should be passed on to the Private Aircraft Owners Association and refueling centers need to be set up in interior locations.

Other details for setting up a autonomous Air Transport Authority and adopting an open skies policy with respect to international airlines, Transport Development. Such changes will provide tourists with more flight connections to visit Guyana and would be of enormous benefit to the sector.

Product Improvement

The following areas of Guyana's tourism product should be improved using the suggested guidelines.

Visitor Security

Visitor security should be an absolute priority through out Guyana. This must be guaranteed on all levels simultaneously; it should include training for the police force on interaction with tourists as well as a permanent police presence in the major thoroughfares of main towns and cities. Street lighting needs to be improved. Procedures on crime reporting should be streamlined to enable the visitor to spend as little time as possible in police stations reporting crimes, and all efforts should be made to make the experience of crime reporting as hassle free and as comfortable as possible.

In addition to education for the police force on dealing with tourists, the best form of visitor protection can be achieved by educating the general public to look out for tourists and their safety and to discourage crimes against tourists within their own communities. This mind set already exists to some extent, as part of the genuine warmth and hospitality that most Guyanese have towards visitors. This attitude needs only to be enhanced through good public awareness campaigns showing how local Guyanese can benefit from tourism and visitor safety.

Due to the fact that certain areas of the interior are open to drug trafficking and other criminal activity (Kaieteur is a prime example), the efforts of the Guyana Defense Force, the police force and tour operators should be coordinated in these areas. Police stations should be set up in areas where tourist activity is high, in particular at Kaieteur Falls, where there have been many reported incidents of theft from tourists.

Search and Rescue

There must be a national search and rescue operation that can deal with all eventualities. This includes high-level detection methods, fast and effective evacuation procedures and top level medical training and equipment. This would require an established mechanism between the Tourism Board, TAG, the Government, the police and the army.

Tour operators must have adequate safety equipment for the tours they conduct. Training in first aid and CPR must be mandatory for all persons/guides conducting or in charge of tourists, and adequate emergency evacuation plans and procedures must be set for all tour operations and resorts. These safety procedures and equipment must be linked to the licensing of these operations, and failure to comply with the minimum safety standards set for the industry should carry severe and enforceable penalties for the failure in their observance.

A list of licensed operators should be made available to all tourists through hotels and other outlets.

Insurance

At present, many resorts, hotels and tour operations within the industry do not have public liability insurance. Steps should be taken to amend laws pertaining to insurance to give the industry access to adequate levels of insurance. In conjunction with this, adequate insurance for all resorts, hotels, charter airlines and tour operations should be made mandatory and linked to the licensing of these operations.

Financial Streamlining

While more retail outlets, restaurants, hotels and tour operations in Georgetown are beginning to accept credit cards, this acceptance is still not widespread in the capital city, let alone nationwide. Travelers' checks are accepted as reliable currency, but since many outlets must wait 28 days for reimbursement, this discourages their use. All necessary steps must be taken to ensure that tourists can get easy access to money and that facilities for changing foreign exchange and travelers checks are widespread and convenient.

Visas

Though there has been a relaxation on visa requirements for visitors to Guyana, pre-travel visa requirements for entry into Guyana should be completely eliminated.

Timehri International Airport

Plans for the expansion and upgrading of Timehri International Airport are underway of this National Development Strategy. With regard to tourism, the airport is in urgent need of fully manned tourist arrival and departure booths. The departure booth will also be a place for lodging complaints about Guyana that should be channeled back to the relevant authorities.

Marketing Guyana as an Eco-tourism Destination

Marketing tourism can be expected to be expensive and the Tourism Board will have to enter into arrangements with the Government and industry to promote generic advertising for the country. As the industry and the economy grow this can be done through a mechanism of matching funds, whereby the Government agrees to match funds pledged by TAG at an agreed ratio, say of 1:2 (industry to Government).

Specific markets must be studied and targeted individually according to their needs and demands. There should be tourism representatives in key cities such as New York, Miami, Toronto, London and Frankfurt. Niche groups such as clubs for bird watching, nature tourism, biodiversity study and conservation that pre-qualify as eco-tourists should be targeted with information on Guyana. The advertising dollar should be carefully spent in appropriate magazines such as those that deal with nature and the environment. The country must also invite writers and specialised tour operators for visits to the national sites as a way of gaining publicity and marketing the product.

Guyana is currently featured in the South American Handbook, but efforts must be made to improve that information, produce more literature on Guyana itself and to include Guyana in a wider range of guide books featuring South American and Caribbean destinations. In addition, the use of existing and up-and-coming technologies should be explored as a way to convey information to the international traveler. While Guyana is marginally listed on the Internet, this facility has to be expanded and upgraded; given the profile of the average eco-tourist, computer based technology is an excellent way to convey information to this segment of the market.

Joint Destination Tourism

Joint destination packages should be developed with neighboring countries. However, this does not mean that Guyana can expect to encourage operators in the Caribbean to send their visitors here. Joint destination tourism is about attracting tourists to Guyana in the first place and encouraging them here by offering them an extension trip to another destination. The industry should work closely with the Board in promoting this.

Regular Bulletin on the Industry

There is need for an adequate system for collecting information on visitor arrivals, visitor activities, and visitor feedback. This information must be collected and collated in a timely manner and must be made public. This would provide the industry with up-to-date information on the market and allow it to see where it stands with respect to overall trends. The published totals would also allow the comparison of figures by different agencies to keep track of the number of tourists that visit Guyana. For instance, the number of tourists that visit Kaieteur National Park can be compared to the number of visitors that are reported visiting there by tour operators. While the published figures would represent totals, figures for individual companies will be open for inspection by tax officials to ensure compliance with reporting requirements.

The bulletin could also include information on the world travel market, such as emerging tastes and visitor preferences. This would allow to Guyana to respond efficiently and effectively to changing patterns.

Regulations and Standards within the Industry

In regulating the industry, the Tourism Board will have the authority to licence operators, resort owners, hoteliers, and other tourism-related operators. The Board will also set minimum standards to be met by those involved in the sector; meeting these standards would also be one of the criteria for obtaining a licence. It is not expected that the Board will itself grade or classify facilities, but this responsibility will be left to independent certifiers. The Board will have the responsibility for writing and monitoring regulations and standards.

To ensure that the tourism industry can deliver on the promises it makes through its marketing campaign, strict standards need to be set within the industry with appropriate penalties for non compliance, particularly standards pertaining to visitor safety and environmental integrity.

Tour Guides

Tour guides are an important part of interior resorts and tour operations. Areas of knowledge should include basic life saving procedures as well as a good information base on the geography of Guyana and the wildlife and eco-systems in the different regions of the country. Of primary importance would be the communication skills of such persons; it is not just what they know, it is the ability to impart it to tourists that matters. The Tourism Board in conjunction with the University of Guyana should develop short courses for tourist guides, and practical training with hoteliers and operators should be pursued. The use of guest lectures from the industry should be actively encouraged.

The Wildlife Trade

Severe restrictions and legislation governing the wildlife trade should be implemented. Breeding of these animals is an alternative for satisfying the needs of tourists and restaurants in Georgetown.

Georgetown

Strict zoning and building codes should be enforced in Georgetown. New buildings in the city should be made to conform to Georgetown's rich architectural heritage. The further construction of concrete buildings along Main Street and Avenue of the Republic should be proscribed.

Continuity of Work in the Sector

Follow-up efforts in the sector, such as the Integrated Eco-tourism Development Plan by the OAS, must build upon the recommendations of this Strategy.

Public Health

The Tourism Board and TAG must work with the Ministry of Health to ensure that an integrated and effective attack is carried out on malaria and other vector-borne diseases.

Legislative Requirements

Establishing the Tourism Board

Legislation needs to be enacted to establish a Tourism Board for the support of the tourism industry. This Board could be established through the Public Corporations Act (1988) or by completely new legislation.

Government Regulations

Following from the laws which establish the Tourism Board, a series of regulations should be prepared to implement those laws. It is not recommended that the regulatory framework of Guyana's tourism legislation should extend, in the present situation, to imposing qualitative classification or grading by law, but eventually that should be a goal.

Services to Tourism

International Transportation

It is recommended that Guyana should replace its applied civil aviation codes with local legislation. However, if resource constraints dictate the continued use of British legislation for Guyana's aviation law, then it is recommended that a least Guyanese legislation should be enacted to give the Minister the choice of when to adopt and apply new British regulations. In this way, the laws can be updated periodically based on trends in the world as reflected in updated British laws.

International Water Transportation

Guyana still depends on the United Kingdom's Merchant Shipping Act of 1894. Since a modern Caribbean-oriented model Shipping Act exists, which has been prepared by CARICOM in conjunction with the Caribbean Law Institute, it is recommended that Guyana should enact this legislation. For Guyana, the main advantage of such legislation would be to give some control of ships in its waters and sports.

Guyana's interest in maritime legisl .tion should not be confined to passenger movements at sea. Maritime pollution could hurt the tourism product through, for example, the depletion of the sea turtles in the northwest. While Guyana is a party to the United Nations Convention on the Law of the Sea, and the Maritime Boundaries Act can be considered to allow for the exploitation of resources through jurisdictional allocation, this Act does not provide for environmental considerations. The fact that Guyana did not sign any of the leading International Maritime Organisation Conventions except the constituent convention, does not auger well for the protection of the marine environment. Guyana should meet international obligations to have legislation in place to safeguard the marine environment under its jurisdiction, and should participate in MARPOL 1973/78 and SOLAS.

With respect to inland water navigation, the River Navigation Act and Regulations and the Fisheries Act should be reviewed with regard to the standards they require for river navigation and to their exemptions of categories of craft from the application of those standards.

Accommodations, Restaurants and Places of Entertainment

General hotels regulation: It is recommended that a system of registration for hotels in the tourist sector be enshrined in law. This system would require that standards be met and maintained as a condition of such registration by the Tourism Board. These standards should be consistent with the best modern industry practice.

Reference to hotels in the laws of Guyana are found in the Provisions Relating to Common Lodging Houses which form a part of the City's by-laws and made under powers contained in the Municipal and District Act. This has certain problems, such as:

1. It relates only to Georgetown,
2. It does not differentiate between hotels, apartments and guest houses, and
3. The standards are outdated.

The Common Lodging House By-Laws apply across the country, but they do not appear to govern hotels. New laws in this area also need to reexamine the minimum number of rooms per hotel that make these liable for payment of the hotel room tax. Consideration should be given to removing the stipulation that only hotels in excess of 15 rooms are liable to pay the tax. Interior resorts should continue to be excluded from the hotel room tax, regardless of the minimum number of rooms they contain so as not to discourage the construction of lodges in the interior.

Protection of Hotels from Visitors' Claims: A good precedent in law to protect hotel owners from claims from visitors is the English Hotel Proprietors' Act of 1956. This law allows an escape from being liable for losses suffered by guests unless they take advantage of the hotel's security system. Reasonable limits for losses are the equivalent of US $100 for any one item and US $200 as the aggregate loss. There should also be legislation to prevent guests who do not pay their hotel bills from leaving Guyana.

Food Licensing and Food Safety: The legislative provisions for hotels and restaurants in Georgetown should be applied countrywide. Although there is provision against the employment of food handlers suffering from infection diseases, it is not clear that the current system of food handlers' permits is legislated. The current system of permits which must be renewed every six months also need to be reviewed, with the intent of extending the validity of the permit. Extending its validity would reduce the logistical problems and expense of bringing food handlers from the interior to Georgetown to be tested. A strengthening of the system of distributing these permits regionally could also be pursued.

Legislation should also be enacted that requires new restaurants and hotels, or those undergoing renovation, to have adequate toilet facilities and amenities for disabled persons.

Places of Entertainment: The preparation of special legislation to regulate places of public entertainment, with rules governing matters such as capacity limitations, provision of sanitary facilities and fire exits, safeguards against noise nuisance, and other offences to neighbouring residents, is recommended. Similarly, legislation is needed that provides in detail the required fire safety criteria, or structural reliability, means of escape, fire-fighting equipment, fire detection, and restriction or suppression of the spread of fire.

Zoning

It would appear that the Town and Country Planning Act provides legal control over zoning and the quality and suitability of the construction of buildings in Georgetown, but these are not enforced. The law should be updated and areas in Georgetown such as Main Street and the Avenue of the Republic should be included. The Act should be amended to provide for its automatic application to newly developed areas.

The designation of a buffer zone of 66 feet inland from the low water mark of creeks as Government reserve should be maintained but legislative allowance should be made for restricted use of such zones by lodges that are adjacent to creeks. This should not prejudice the use of the zone for access.

Building Codes and Tourism Facilities

Building codes for interior lodges can be expected to vary from those for structures built from established building materials. It is impractical to develop codes for interior resorts because of the new and multitudinous indigenous materials that may legitimately be used. The use of such materials is necessary if lodges are going to fit into the surrounding environment. Lodges must, however, be certified by a professional engineer.

There must also be minimum standards legislated for the disposal of sewerage and garbage. These should be included in the requirements for environmental impact statements for tourist facilities in the interior.

There should also be regulations for the distance between tourism lodges and buffer zones around lodges, etc.

National Parks

It is intended that legislation covering the establishment of National Parks and Protected Areas will be written as Guyana moves to establish a Protected Areas System. The new law should replace the Kaieteur National Park Act (Cap. 20:02) and National Parks Commission Act (1977-23). The powers of the Guyana Forestry Commission "to identify, establish, maintain and manage forests including national parks, wildlife areas, and natural reserves" should be removed from the Commission and place under the authority established to regulate National Parks.

The National Trust Act (Cap. 20:03) provides for the protection of national monuments but this needs adequate enforcement.

Protection of Wildlife and Fisheries

The Fisheries Act (Cap. 78:01) and accompanying Fisheries Aquatic Wild Life Regulations and the Wild Birds Protection Act (Cap. 71:01) allow for some protection of fisheries and birds. The scope of the Fisheries Act is not confined to fauna but is wide enough to include the protection of both marine and fresh water aquatic flora, as the result of the amendment of the Act in 1977.

Between these two acts, four-footed wildlife is excluded. The Wild Life Protection Act of 1987, which should have remedied this situation, is still not enacted. This Act should be enacted.

The Environmental Protection Act

The recent enactment of the Environmental Protection Bill should be followed expeditiously by the drafting of suitable regulations for the implementation of its various prescriptions.

Appendix 1-A: Typical offering in the Guyanese Tourism Industry

Company	Barakara Island	Emerald tower	The gazebo	Karanambu	Rockview	Shanklands	Timberhead
				Resorts			
Resort location	Mazaruni River	Madawini Creek Linden Highway	Kaow Island, Essequibo	North Rupununi	Annai, North Rupununi	Essequibo River	Pokerero River
Land area (acres)		165	136	125 square miles	+/- 3	96	15
Land tenures		25 yr. lease from Lands & Surveys	Transport land	25 year lease from Lands & Surveys	Amerindian or State has permission from both	Transport Land	Lease from Santa Amerindian Reservation
Activities	Swimming, volley ball, jet skies, jet boat tours to surrounding nature spots. Caters for groups, individuals, conference facilities	Swimming, Boats, fishing, cycling, walking, bird watching, miniature golf, table tennis, conference facilities	Trails, fishing, water sports, swimming, sauna, visit to nearby historical sites	Boat trips, bird watching, trekking, fishing, Amerindian villages	Pony trekking, bird watching and nature tours, fishing, Amerindian villages, visit to Iwokrama	Jungle walks, water sports, boat tours to surrounding areas, croquet, golf	Day & Evening jungle walks and boat tours, cayman watching, bird watching, canoeing, swimming, volleyball and badminton.

Cost all inclusive	G $8 000 (Day trip)	US $ 85 (day trip) US $ 155-245 o/n	US $ 120 per person o/n plus cost of transportation	US $ 120	US $ 95 - 115	US $ 125	US $90 (Day Trip) US $ 145 (Overnight)
Target group	Overseas Business and holidays, local	overseas, local and overseas business persons. Expats based in Guyana	overseas: holiday and business	not specified	Guyanese, Brazilian, Overseas	Overseas and Local	Mainly overseas business persons and tourists, some local tourists
Start date	1995	19/09/92	late 1989	1989	April 1993	May 1992	May 1991
Capacity		16-26	12	10	8	16-25	20
Expansion plans		More resorts planned in the Interior. Head Falls resort opening	Yes	No	Yes, up to 20 persons	Yes - more cottages	Yes
Primary land use	Tourism	Tourism	Saw milling	Cattle ranching	Ranching and Farming	Tourism	Tourism
Government Liaison	Min. Of Trade & Tourism Lands & Surveys	Min. of Trade & Tourism Min. Of Finance	Min. of Trade; Guyana Natural Resources Agency	Min. of Trade & Tourism	Min. of Trade & Tourism	Min. of Trade & Tourism	Mins. of Trade & Tourism, Finance, Foreign Affairs

Appendix 1-B: Typical Offering in the Guyanese Tourism Industry

Hotels

Hotel	Ariantze	Cara Lodge	Cara Suites	Embassy Club	Park Hotel	Campala Hotel	Pegasus Hotel	Queenstown Inn	Hotel Tower
Location	176 Middle Street	293, Quamina Street	176, Middle Street	Pere Street	37, Main Street	10, Camp Street	Seawall Road	65, Anira & Peter Rose	74-75 Main Street
Rooms	8	14	15	22	45	22	134	6	56
Facilities	1,2,4,5,6,8,10	1,2,4,5,6,7,8	1,2,4,5,6,7,8	1,2,3,4,5,6,7,8,9	1,2,5,6,7,4,8	1,2,5,6	1,2,3,4,5,6,7,8,9	1,2,5,6	1,2,3,4,5,6,7,8,9
Target Group	Corporate	Business, leisure	Business	Business	Business/Group Delegations	Business	Corporate/Business	Business/Locals	Business
Amerindian Involvement		Yes, family live there and run facilities	Yes, employed on site.	Yes, employed on site and visit Amerindian villages	Yes, employment, support from council		None, except support local schools and help out in emergencies		Yes, employment and close links with villages of Santa

Cost	$55	$ 85-130	$87- 145	$80-130	$ 40- 60	$61- 82	$ 110-260	$55-80	$85- 160
Start Date	1991	1996	1995	1994	1893	1988	1969	1994	circa 1866
Expans-ion Plans	Rooms 3-4 Rooms	Rooms 2 Executive Rooms	None	Create an interior resort	Yes	Upgrading facilities	None	None	14 Deluxe Rooms
Govt. Liasion	Min. of Trade	Min. of Trade Min. of Finance	Min. of Trade Min. of Finance	Min. of Trade	Min. of Trade Min. of Finance	None	Min. of Trade Min. of Fin. Min. of F. A.	Min. of Trade	None

Services and Facilities

1. Private Bath/ Shower, 2. Air Conditioning, 3. Swimming Pool, 4. Restaurant, 5. Telephone, 6.Television, 7. Business Center, 8. Bar, 9. Gym, 10. Night Club

Appendix 1-C
Typical Offering in the Guyanese Tourism Industry

Tour Operators

Company	Cattelya Rainforest	Cortours	Discover Tours	Shell Beach Adventures	White Water Adventures	Wilderness Explorers	Wonderland Tours
Location of Tours	Kaitieur, Essequibo Region, Bartica,	Orealla - Manituba, Corentyne River	Kaiteur, Orinduik Emerald	Shell Beach, Kaieteur/ Orinduik, Essequibo	Mazaruni	Comprehensive standard custom designed	Kaiteur & Orinduik, Santa Mission,

	Bartica, Linden	River	Tower	Essequibo and personalised activities anywhere.		designed itineraries to all areas of Guyana	Mission, Essequibo, Mazaruni, G/T city tour, Berbice, Linden
Activities	City Tours, Overland trips, Nature walks, Trekking, fishing	Boat Tours, hiking (3-5 days)	Bird watching, Overland Camping, River Tours, Kaiteur & Orinduik	Kaiteur & Orinduik Falls by air, Rupununi Ranches & Kaiteur	Inland river trips	Nature and adventure based activities such as bird watching, wildlife watching, hiking, canoeing, horse trekking, history tours and cultural tours	Essequibo Fiver, Santa Mission, Kaiteur & Orinduik
Cost Range	$20 (City) $150/day (1-7 days)	$8140 - $800/day	$175/day	$50 - $170	$60 US (G$8000) incl. Day trip $120 US(G$16 800) o/n trip	From US$30 7 days - US$1,140 14 days- US$2,095	$25-300

Target Group	Local (w/discount) regional (W.I.) Germans &British	Intl. mostly	Local & Intl.	Local & Intl.	Local, overseas, business	International, regional and local	Overseas Guyanese
Start Date	1994, April		1974	1995, April	1995, March	1 August, 1994	1989
Group Size Min- Max	2-12	3-15	8- no maximum	4 - no max.	15-40	Minimum 1 person. No maximum	2-60
Expansion Plans	Resort site in Santa Mission	Building camps in Manituba	Great falls	Not Immediately	More Cabins (private) on island	Nature resort and itineraries to new areas	Shell Beach Overland Kamarang & area
Govt. Liasion	Min. of Trade	Min. of Trade		Min. of Trade / Min. of A.A.	Min. of Trade	Min. of Trade; Min. of Amerindian Affairs	No liaison
Amerindian Involvement	Amer. Boat guide; family inside mission, also overseas site	Very little, other than visiting settlements	Work sites run by Amerindians	All Amerindian involvement - family full time at Shell Beach - guides, drivers etc.	Amerindian staff on site and in Georgetown	Partnership with some Amerindian communities to conduct tours. Others employed for tours as necessary.	Interior - hired on freelance basis

Appendix 2-A
Visitor Arrivals by Country of Origin 1992-1994

Country	1992	1993	1994	% Share 1994
USA	34566	57269	42143	37.4
Canada	13976	no data	17668	15.7
Europe	6763	7892	8104	7.2
Caribbean	14427	19514	21916	19.4
South America	5149	20553	20904	18.5
Other	no data	1899	2016	1.8
Total	74881	107127	112751	100

Appendix 2-B
Monthly Arrivals of Visitors 1992-1994

Month	1992	1993	1994
January	4562	6251	7513
February	5463	7039	7322
March	4994	7567	9330
April	5990	8169	7974
May	5122	6933	6629
June	5261	8320	8278
July	9699	13972	14760
August	9136	12345	14692
September	4594	7233	7550
October	4538	7203	6715
November	5127	7236	6924
December	10395	14959	15064
TOTAL	74881	107227	112751

Source: Caribbean Tourism Organisation, Caribbean Tourism Statistical Report 1993; 1994

TOURISM POLICY: A CASE STUDY OF INDIA

The World Scenario and India's Position

In recent years tourism has emerged as a major economic activity that is employment oriented and earns foreign exchange. Its share in the worlds GDP in 1994-95 was 10 per cent which is more than the world military budgets put together. In global terms, the investment in tourism industry and travel trade accounts for 7 per cent of the total capital investment. Today 21.2 crore people around the globe are employed in travel trade and tourism. In future, this industry is likely to see unprecedented growth. According to the World Tourism Council at Bruseels, the revenues from travel and tourism in Asia Pacific region will grow at the rate of 7.8 per cent annually over the next decade.

Amongst the economic sectors, the tourism sector is highly labor intensive. A survey by the Government of India notes that the rate of employment generation (direct and indirect) in tourism is 52 persons employed per Rs.10 lakh investment (based on 1992-93 Consumer Price Index). This is much higher than the rates of employment generation in most other economic sectors.

India's tourism industry has also recorded phenomenal growth. The rate of international arrivals in India in recent years has been to the tune of about 19 lakh arrivals per year. The unprecedented growth in tourism in India has made it the third largest foreign exchange earner after gem and jewellery and ready-made garments. This is not surprising since India possesses a whole range of attractive normally sought by tourists and which includes natural attractions like landscapes, scenic beauty, mountains, wildlife, beaches, kajor rivers and manmade attractions such as monuments, forts, palaces and havelis. However, in global terms, inspite of such attractions, tourist arrivals in India are a mere 0.30 per cent of the world arrivals. Receipts are similarly low, just a 0.50 per cent of the world receipts. We are still quite far from the target of 50 lakh tourist arrivals per year.

Tourism in the Gujarat

A separate Tourism Department was established in 1973 to identify and develop the tourism potential in the State. This was followed by the creation of Tourism Corporation of Gujarat

Limited in 1978 which was entrusted with the task of undertaking and developing tourism-related commercial activities. The Corporation is presently engaged in a variety of activities such as creation of lodging and boarding facilities for the tourists and other aspects of tourist acilitation such as transportation, packaged tours, wayside catering along the National and State Highways, arranging cultural festivals, organizing exhibitions and producing and distributing maps, posters, brochures and pamphlets. The Corporation has set up accommodation facilities at Chorwad, Ahmedpur Mandvi, Porbandar, Veraval, Hajira, Ubharat and Tithal. Similar facilities at pilgrimage centres like Palitana, Somnath, Dwarkja, Pavagadh and Dakor have also been set up by the Corporation. One of the recent tourist attractions introduced by the Corporation in collaboration with the Indian Railways is a special tourist train. The Royal Orient Train which connects up various tourist destinations straddling the Gujarat and Rajasthan State. However, the Corporation has suffered losses due to a number of organisational constraints. In order to minimize these losses and also to provide better services to the tourists, the Government has undertaken privatisation of some of the commercial property units of the Corporation.

In spite of possessing a variety of tourist attractions such as wildlife, scenic beauty, pilgrimage centres, exotic traditional crafts and festivals, beaches, hospitality of the region and a varied healthy and tasteful cuisine, the State has not been able to accelerate the pace of tourism in comparison to other states. In 1991, the State did declare a tourism policy but it did not elicit adequate response from the private sector since the policy contained only a handful of benefits while the implementation was tardy due to legal and administrative constraints. This was at a time when the Government of India had already declared tourism as an industry and a large number of states had followed suit. This enabled the tourism industry to avail of incentives, reliefs, benefits available to the industry in those states.

While other state Governments made successful efforts in developing tourism within their states, the relative inability of the Gujarat State to harness and develop its full tourist potential may be attributed to a combination of factors such as lack of effective policies, inadequate infrastructure, ineffective marketing and lack of decent facilities for the tourists.

The main rationale for formulating a comprehensive tourism policy is rooted, on one hand, in the convergence of socio-economic spread benefits, environment—friendliness and employment potential of tourism industry and on the other, in the growing demand for tourism products in the State, brought by a rapid industrial growth in the State during the recent years that has led to tremendous increase in number of business travellers.

Objectives

The main objective of the Gujarat States Tourism Policy will be to undertake intensive development of tourism in the State and thereby increase employment opportunities. The following related objectives are dovetailed with main objectives

- Identify and develop tourist destinations and related activities.
- Diversifications of tourism products in order to attract more tourists through a varied consumer choice.
- Comprehensive development of pilgrimage centres as tourist destinations.
- Create adequate facilities for budget tourists.
- Strengthen the existing infrastructure and develop new ones where necessary.
- Creation of tourism infrastructure so as to preserve handicrafts, folk arts and culture of the state and thereby attract more tourists.

Approach and Strategy

In addition to the facilitation role assigned to itself by the Government in the development of tourism, the Government will adopt the following strategy towards the private sector with the objective of securing its active involvement in leading the development of tourism in the State.

- The tourism will be given the status of industry in order that the facilities and benefits available to the industry are also made available to tourism projects.

- A special incentives package will be made available for encouraging new tourism projects as well as expansion of existing tourism units.

- Infrastructural facilities will be strengthened and developed within the State, particularly in Special Tourism Areas which will be notified latter and which will be developed by adopting an integrated-area.

- Effective mechanisms will be set up to build meaningful co-ordination with the Central Government and the State Governments agencies, the local self-government bodies and the NGOs.

- Government will encourage building effective linkages with the relevant economic agents and agencies such as the national and international tour operators and travel agents of repute, hotel chains and global institutions connected with tourism such as WTO.

Policy Proposals

Tourism as Industry

Like other industrial projects, tourism projects too involve professional management, capital investment, special skills and training. The Government of India and a number of other states have declared tourism as an industry. Gujarat State which is at the forefront of the industrial development will also declare tourism as an industry. This will enable the tourism projects to be reliable to get benefits contained.

Availability of land is a primary requirement of any project. The process of grant of land will be facilitated in urban areas for the projects concerning setting up of hotels, restaurants and apartment hotels etc.

Existing arrangements for grant of government waste land to industrial units will be made applicable to various tourism projects.

Arrangements will be made to acquire private land under Land Acquisition Act for various tourism projects by companies registered under the Companies Act.

The existing commercial rates of NA assessment applicable to land involving tourism projects would be reviewed and rates of NA assessment for industrial purposes will be made applicable to them.

As one of the sets of infrastructural institutions, the State Financial Institutions have made an important contribution in creating conductive environment for industrial entrepreneurs. They will be called upon to do the same for tourism entrepreneurs in terms of making available adequate finance.

So far, the lending from the State Financial Institutions has been largely confined to hotels only. In reality, the range of activities for tourism projects is far larger than just hotels as can be seen from the following illustrative list:

Accommodation Projects

- Hotels
- Resorts
- Motels
- Apartment Hotels
- Heritage Hotels

Food Oriented Projects

- Restaurants
- Wayside Facilities on the State Highways.

Other Tourism Related Projects

- Amusement Parks and Water Sports

- Handicraft Village Complexes
- Fairs and Festivals
- Camps and Facilities Encouraging Adventure
- Train Travel Projects
- Sea/RiverCruise Projects
- Sound and Light Shows
- Museums
- Natural Parks/Zoos
- Safari Projects
- Ropeways
- Sports/Health Facilities Complexes
- Training Schools for the managerial expertise for Hospitality Industry
- Golf Courses

Service Oriented Projects

- Travel Agency
- Tour Operation
- Transport Operation
- Linkage with the International Hotel Chains (Franchise)
- Human Resources Development (HRD) for Tourism Industry and necessary training facilities.

Most of the projects on this illustrative list are not eligible for loans from the banks or the State Financial Agencies. It will be necessary to make suitable changes in the lending criteria for viable projects in the listed activities in order than their financial requirements are met.

The modification of the lending criteria of the State Financial Agencies will be made with regard to the financial ceiling, debt equity ratio, recovery period, moratorium etc.

Necessary arrangements will be made to ensure that the State Financial Agencies and the banks attach adequate priority to the financing requirements of tourism projects.

As referred earlier, a new incentive package will be made available to replace the existing incentive policy instituted in 1991. A tax holiday of 5-10 years in respect of following taxes will be made available upto 100 per cent of capital investment to various tourism projects located in Special Tourism Areas whether declared by the Central Government or the State Government, located in designated areas and located on National and State Highways. The scope and the extent of the benefits of tax holiday will vary according to certain considerations such as the admissible expenditure, the size of the capital investment etc. The benefit of tax holiday will also be made available for the purpose of expansion of the existing tourism projects in these areas:

- SalesTax
- Purchase Tax
- Electricity Duty
- Luxury Tax
- Entertainment Tax

Necessary administrative arrangements will be made at the State and District Level to operationalize the incentive schemes.

Suitable schemes will be designed to market tourism products, and particularly wide publicity will be secured in respect of various facilities being offered by the travel agents, tour operators etc.

Special paying guest scheme will be formulated for providing adequate and inexpensive lodging and boarding facilities too take care of seasonal flows of tourists to the pilgrimage centres during festivals.

Financial assistance will be provided for the preparation of feasibility reports by consultants in respect of tourism projects.

Structure of the taxes and tariffs, *e.g.* luxury tax, entertainment tax, sales tax, etc., will be reviewed with reference to developmental needs of tourism sector and necessary amendments will be made.

Redefining the Roles of the State and the Market

Since the approach of the Tourism Policy focuses on market-led developments, the role of the State would be as follows:

The Government proposes to make commercial services available entirely through private sector or in association with it. The States role will primarily focus on strengthening and upgrading existing infrastructure and development of new infrastructure. Reputed consultants will be hired to prepare area development master plans/feasibility studies in respect of important tourist destinations and areas of tourism potential, *e.g.* Sardar Sarovar Project Area, Kutch, Beach sites and area covering Porbandar, Gir Forest, Veraval, Somnath, Ahmedpur-Mandvi, Saputara, Modhera etc.

Efforts will be made to get funding for development of infrastructure for these destinations/areas from national and international agencies.

To ensure timely provision of necessary funding, the Government will earmark funds in the annual budgets of the departments concerned for securing the purpose.

In conformity with States promotional role in the development of tourism sector, all competitive and commercial activities of Tourism Corporation of Gujarat Limited will be privatised except where no entrepreneur is coming forward to meet the existing need. This privatisation would help strengthen the financial position of the corporation and also help provide qualitative services to the tourists.

Tourism Corporation of Gujarat Limited will assume a catalytic role focused on acting as clearing house of information, production and distribution of promotional literature, policy advice etc.

The Tourism Corporation will assist entrepreneurs and agencies in tourism sector and will try to help alleviate their difficulties particularly vis-à-vis the Government and its agencies.

A Computerized Information Centre will be set up at the State level to make available necessary information to the agencies/entrepreneurs who wish to set up tourism projects.

In addition to its existing offices in Mumbai, Delhi and Chennai, the Tourism Corporation will also open its offices in other major cities of India to give wide publicity and disseminate information on Gujarat Tourism and market tourism products through these offices and through reputed travel agents in other big cities. Thus, the information about Gujarats tourist destinations and related information would be made available to tourists from outside the State in their own cities.

There is already a scheme of 50 per cent matching grant from the State Government to the local self-governing bodies for the development of local tourist destinations. This scheme will be made more effective and attractive and necessary provisions in the budget will be made. This will help centralize the process of developing tourist destinations.

The process of decentralization will be further strengthened by delegation of administrative and executive powers of approval of incentives to small tourism projects to District Level Bodies headed by the Collector. These bodies, in addition, will also secure co-ordination from other departments/agencies of the Government in development and promotion of tourism. Representation will be given on this body to the experts, individual agencies and individuals connected with the tourism.

A Single window clearance system will be instituted for speedy clearance of various permissions, approvals required under different laws and rules. Necessary modification/amendment will be made to various administrative arrangements and laws which are not consistent with the approach of this Policy. Care will be taken to ensure that prospective investors do not have to suffer protracted and complex administrative process.

Intensive efforts will be undertaken to attract investors from outside the State as well as from other countries including non-resident Indians to invest in tourism sector on large scale. Tourism Corporation of Gujarat Limited and Directorate of Tourism will play active role to ensure that investors get various permissions easily and are provided with all the necessary facilities.

A High Powered Committee under the Chairmanship of Chief Secretary with Director of Tourism as the Member Secretary will be constituted with the objective of securing effective co-ordination among various Government departments and agencies as also to speed up decision making proceeds concerning tourism. The committee will meet regularly and enjoy full powers of Government, provided the approval of the Chief Minister and the Council of Ministers will be obtained wherever required.

In order to create a participate forum for deliberation and discussion concerning tourism industry, a Tourism Advisory Council headed by the Chief Minister will be set up. The Ministers and Secretaries of administrative departments concerned will be the members. The representatives of tourism industry, experts and related organisations will be nominated as members. The Additional Chief Secretary (Tourism) will be the Member Secretary of this Council.

The Council will meet periodically to deliberate upon policy as well as individual issues and offer suitable advice to the Government.

Perspective Planning

Perspective plan for tourism development will be prepared in consultation with experts. An overview of possible tourism products is offered below:

Religious (Pilgrimage) and Archaeological Tourism

Gujarat has a preponderance of pilgrimage centers as in some other states. Somnath and Dwarka—some of the well known and revered sites of ancient Hindu temples are situated in the State. The temple architecture has reached heights of excellence in Jain temples at Shetrunji, Girnar and Taranga. The temple of Ambaji situated in Aravalli range in North Gujarat is an important religious centre for devotees in the country. Dakor,

Pavagadh, Bahucharaji, Shamlaji, Narayan Sarovar, Sudamas Porbandar, Kabirvad Shuklatirth, Kayavarohan, Bhadrakali Temple Ahmedabad and Tankara—Maharshi Dayanand Saraswatis birth place are also important pilgrimage destinations which have kept alive the religious sentiments of the people. Lakhs of pilgrims visit these places every year.

These places are visited not only by the devotees from all over the country but also by non-resident Indians and travellers especially from the eastern part of the world. Necessary accommodation facilities and related services will be created on these sites. For ensuring orderly and planned development of pilgrimage centres, the State Government has constituted Pavitra Dham Vikas Board chaired by the Chief Minister. The Board will prepare and implement plans to provide necessary facilities to the devotees and also ensure conservation of cultural atmosphere consistent with sentiments of visiting devotees.

Shamlaji is an ancient site for Buddhists. The excavated relies of Buddhist period at the site are now kept in a museum at Baroda.

There are a number of places of archaeological importance is such as the temple-town of Palitana, Modhera with its Sun temple, historical Ranki Vav at Patan with relics of an ancient capital, the Girnar Hills with Hindu and Jain temples, Junagadh with a historical fort, Dabhoi, Champaner, Pavagadh, Shaking Minarets, Gandhi Ashram, Siddi Sayed Jali etc. These can be developed by providing necessary infrastructural facilities and marketed as tourist destinations to attract tourists.

Heritage Tourism

A large number of old palaces, havelis, darbargadhs exist in the State. These historical buildings can be converted into hotels, restaurants or museums by providing suitable incentives to owners. Wildlife and Pilgrimage Tourism circuits can be linked to heritage properties exploiting the geographical congruity. Development of this sub-sector will not only attract foreign tourists but also provide encouragement and support to local art and craft.

Government will take necessary steps to promote Heritage tourism in the State.

Wildlife Tourism

There is substantial scope for development of tourism based on wildlife in the State. Gir Forest of Gujarat is the last stronghold of Asiatic Lions. The Bear Sanctuary at Ratan Mahal (Dist. Panchmahal), Black Buck Sanctuary at Velavadar (Dist. Bhavnagar), Bird Sanctuary at Nalsarovar (Dist. Ahmedabad), Wild Ass Sanctuary at Kutch etc. can be effectively developed into tourist destinations by providing infrastructural facilities. In order to facilitate visitors to these areas, coordination among various agencies will be established.

Coastal and Beach Tourism

The Gujarat State has the longest coastline among Maritime States of the country. Identified stretches of coastline can be developed into beaches from tourism point of view. It will be the endeavour of the State to develop beach potential by providing such facilities as may attract foreign tourists.

Various tourist destinations easily accessible from the coast will be linked through coastal shipping circuits.

Tourism based on Traditional Art and Craft and Cultural Activities

Banni in Kutch, Khambhat, Junagadh etc. are known for their craftsmanship. Similarly, there are hundreds of fairs that are celebrated through out the year with enthusiasm. Tarnetar Fair in Surendranagar District, Chitra Vichitra Fair at Poshina (Sabarkantha District), Kanwat Fair at Chhota Udepur (Panchmahals District), Dang Darbar in Dang. Bhavnath Fair of Junagadh, Vautha Fair of Ahmedabad etc. have immense tourism value. By developing accommodation, transport and other facilities, these fairs and festivals will be promoted nationally and internationally. The places of importance from art and craft point of view will be included in the tourist circuits and necessary facilities provided to tourists.

Corporate Tourism

Private sector will be encouraged to build the state of the art convention centres, seminar halls etc. so as to attract corporate events like seminar, workshops and annual general meetings. Participants in such events generally have high purchasing power and provide a boost to local economy.

Adventure Tourism

This is also a territory with possibility of development as a sub-sector which will be examined and new activities like Camel Safari in Kutch, Horse-riding in Aravalli hill ranges, Parachuting in Saputara, Trekking in Dang, Pavagadh, Palitana etc. will be promoted. Such activities will create large scale employment opportunities for guides, coolies, traders for hire of tents and equipments etc. and will also encourage paying guest accommodation in such areas. Private entrepreneurs and institutions will be encouraged to develop such facilities.

Highway Tourism

There is a good network of State and National highways which criss-cross the State and a large number of travellers prefer road journey. Because of large geographical expanse of the State, these journeys tend to be quite long and boridng. There is a need for creating necessary facilities like hotels, restaurants, picnic spots, water parks etc. along the highways at suitable intervals for the highway travellers to relax. In fact, travellers can be induced to follow certain traffic routes if such facilities are better developed. Highway facilities and wayside amenities are so well developed in some states that this has become the mainstay of tourism. State shall encourage private investors to create such facilities on highways.

Various sub-sectors of tourism activities listed above will be encouraged by marking new tourism units eligible for incentives under Tax Holiday incentive scheme in designated areas.

As mentioned earlier, the State Government intends to designate certain areas having significant tourist potential as Special Tourism Areas. To this end, reputed consultants and institutions will be engaged to prepare area development plans in respect of various areas such as Kutch District, areas around Sardar Sarovar project area, South Saurashtra areas covering Gir, Porbandar, Veraval, Somnath, beaches and areas of pilgrimage/heritage towns. These areas will be developed by following integrated area development approach. The State Government will make efforts to tap all the source of national and international funding for development of these areas and provide special encouragement to tourism projects being established therein. For ensuring faster development of these areas, area development committees will be constituted.

Human Resources Development

Human Resources Development is an important aspect of service industries. Tourists depend upon travel agents, guides and hence trained manpower is a sine qua non of tourism industry. On the basis of available statistics, training facilities can be safely said to be totally inadequate. If trained manpower is not available locally, the objective of local employment will not be achieved.

Keeping in view the approach of market-led development, the State Government will encourage and support creation of training facilities in the private sector by private agencies/individuals.

Hotel Management course, courses meant for guides, caterer and other supervisory and non-supervisory staff of hotel will be introduced in Industrial Training Institutes (ITIs). Approved hotel associations and private entrepreneurs will be encouraged to create new training facilities by making available land to them for this purpose and by giving other appropriate incentives. The Government will consider setting up a Hotel Management Training Institute at the State level preferably in private sector.

Residents of Gujarat, especially local youths, would be encouraged and facilitated to take part in such training courses.

The Institute of Hotel Management, Catering and Nutrition which is working under the administrative control of the Central Government will be utilized to start new training courses so that the residents of Gujarat can get admission and manpower requirement of this sector is met.

The residents of Gujarat undergoing such training will be reimbursed a part of the tuition fees through scholarships.

Feedback and Monitoring

To make the New Tourism Policy result oriented, implementation will be monitored by a High Powered Committee under the Chairmanship of Chief Secretary.

A Management Information System will be set up to assist the Committee to make available information on various aspects of implementation on a continuous basis. The Committee will also review the policy from time to time.

ANDHRA PRADESH TOURISM POLICY: A CASE STUDY

The Travel and Tourism industry is well on its way tobecoming one of the most powerful growth engines in the coming millennium and is anticipated to generate nearly 338 million jobs by the year 2005 with an annual growth rate of 4.8 per cent.

Acknowledging the vast potential and spin-off tourism has on other industries, the Government of Andhra Pradesh is focusing on tourism for generating greater employment and achieving higher economic growth.

We have a vision of making Andhra Pradesh the destination state of India, given its attractive diversity, natural endowments and friendly population. Andhra Pradesh has a rich tourist potential, which is yet to be exploited. "Bring the world to Andhra Pradesh, take Andhra Pradesh to the world", is our guiding spirit.

Andhra Pradesh has great potential for tourism with its temple towns, beach resorts, monuments and other tourist attractions. Hyderabad and Visakhapatnam airports are proposed to be expanded to receive international flights. Hyderabad has been identified as one of the 5 locations in the country for the establishment of a full-fledged international airport. Direct flights to Singapore have recently commenced from Hyderabad in addition to other destinations. Hyderabad is being developed as a major transit hub between Europe and the far East.

"Andhra Pradesh Unlimited", is the strategy of this policy. We recognize the advantage of offering the collective attractiveness of other places in the region with places in Andhra Pradesh. We plan to decentralize tourism development to districts and local bodies. This policy will also encourage private sector in the tourism industry and provide a frame work for private-public partnership.

To encourage private investment in tourism and related industry, various incentives and concessions are being offered. In keeping with our objective and spirit, taxation has been attempted to be rationalized on the logic of intelligent taxation to enable private sector to expand tourism. While acknowledging the primacy of the private sector, the state retains with itself the responsibility of provision of public goods and for addressing issues related to safety, quality and regulation.

We view this new tourism policy as the product of a shared vision for the state. A series of consultations within the government and with the industry culminated in this policy, which stands enriched by the inputs of the industry. It is necessary that the state moves in a clear direction and consolidates its comparative advantage and realizes its tourist potential to the fullest. It is in this context that the tourism policy has to be evaluated.

Step Forward to the Next Milinium

Tourism Policies are products of time, technology and needs of people. Secular growth trends in tourism witnessed all over are a result of social factors that boost demand for tourism and development in technology. Demand for tourism is propelled mainly by growth. Growing wealth and the rise of a middle class creates that demand. Technology, in turn, makes travel better, easier and hassle-free. Service technology makes leisure an activity which delivers memorable experiences.

Tourism provides opportunity for economic growth, employment generation and poverty alleviation. Tourism holds the key for creation of rural wealth, opportunity for the hitherto neglected segments of society, artisans and service providers in the backward areas. This sector employs 212 million people world wide, generates $3.4 trillion in gross output and contributes $655 billion towards government tax revenues. Travel and Tourism is the world's largest industry. By 2005, the industry is expected to grow to $7 trillion. The industry accounts for 10.7 per cent of the global work force and provides 1 in every 9 jobs. Between the years 1995 and 2000, the industry is adding a new job every 2.5 seconds. Andhra Pradesh is gearing itself for these opportunities with this policy.

This policy, while defining the direction of tourism development and providing a strategic action plan converging on 'Vision 2020' of the state, also articulates the express desire of the state to use it as a growth platform and charter a growth path which is sustainable and responsible. Sustainable because our people, history, culture and life styles are at the core of this policy. We accept competition as the driving force. We also accept our shared vision of protecting our common heritage and not straining our resources when they are fragile. Responsible because this policy defines responsibility of the state, private sector, people and tourists. Moreover, it is designed to be an instrument or a frame work which will enable the state to catapult into a different platform and enable much needed private capital to flow into activities involving technology and enterprise. Eventually, together with the private sector, a champion will be created.

Objectives

- To position tourism as a major growth engine and to harness its direct and multiplier effect for employment generation, economic growth and poverty alleviation in the state of Andhra Pradesh in an environmentally sustainable manner.

- To position Andhra Pradesh as the destination state of India and take advantage of the burgeoning travel and trade market on the demand side and vast untapped potential in heritage, pilgrimage, conventions and beach tourism on the supply side.

- To acknowledge the primacy of the role of the private sector with the government working as the facilitator and the catalyst.

- To bring into effect a co-operative endeavour of both public and private sectors on one hand and between and among different sectors of the government on the other.

- To reap the benefit of the increasing inter-relatedness of the world, which allows capital to move freely across countries and travellers, to cross borders for the benefit of the common man seeking wholesome, memorable and pleasurable experiences.

- To position tourist and tourism-friendly policies as a showcase to demonstrate the attractiveness of Andhra Pradesh as a destination as well as a fast developing business hub.

In the spirit of co-operative federalism, the efforts of the state will augment tourist arrivals in the country and provide larger opportunities for a win-win framework of operation, both among the states and between the federal government and the state of Andhra Pradesh rather than relying on imperial harmonisation strategies. The policy's guiding spirit is: Bring the World to Andhra Pradesh and Take Andhra Pradesh to the World.

The Way Ahead: Where We Are and Where We Want to Be

The reform process has been in motion since 1991. Currently, India's near-complete integration with the global economy is witnessing:

- An upsurge with private capital in the forefront and government playing the crucial role of facilitator and catalyst.
- A fresh and meaningful look at the opportunities of travel, hospitality and leisure market which are growing rapidly.
- There is a growing realisation that private investment should play a larger part in the constructive co-operation between private and public sectors in tourism development. Besides, when a market for leisure and tourism exists, there is a need for affirmative action to tap the market.

This new growth and conducive environment ought to have attracted sizeable private investments to the tourism sector of Andhra Pradesh, with its rich and varied heritage, an array of flora and fauna, and an extensive coast line of nearly 1000 kms. Tourism was declared as an industry in the state as far back as 1986, duly extending benefits and concessions to investors. In 1994, special tourist centers were notified and an incentive subsidy, tax concessions and electricity rebates were offered. The State Tourism Policy was documented and released in 1994. Despite all this, not too much progress has been made in attracting tourists and investors. This could be attributed mainly to low initial development, failure of the state to address the critical areas for kick-starting the tourism development in the state and poor marketing strategies to attract tourists and potential investors.

Tourism is emerging as the fastest growing industry all over the world with the potential to generate one of the highest returns on investments and providing large employment opportunities. Tourism is the second largest foreign exchange earner in the country even though India has a share as low as 0.4 per cent of world tourism with nearly 2.4 million international tourists arriving in 1997. Its importance can therefore be overlooked only at the cost of long-term possibilities.

Tourism is a sector with a tremendous multiplier effect in employment generation and has been a platform from which poverty can be combated and economic growth attained.

Some facts and figures are:

- In India alone, nearly 20.5 million jobs are in the tourism sector.
- Tourism creates 85 jobs with 47 direct against 13 direct in the manufacturing sector with every million rupees spent.
- Consequently, it has become necessary to have a re-look at the existing Tourism Policy parameters as well as to calibrate them to the need of the hour, with a view to attract sizeable private investment in the state, position the state in the travel and tourism market and to promote Andhra Pradesh as a destination state in India. While the potential of tourism as an invisible foreign exchange earner is undoubtedly an important consideration, it is its multiplier effect in large employment creation, its ability in bootstrapping economic growth and fostering poverty alleviation that makes it a prime candidate for governmental focus. India's inability to exploit a burgeoning market in tourism is a pointer to the fact that "imperial harmonisation" of planned development is hardly the recipe for tourism promotion. Federal policies supplemented by focused, aggressive and market friendly approaches of the state are steps in the right direction.

Economic reforms and India's attempt to take the position in an inter-related world has created the right backdrop for the growth of tourism. Firstly, it is liberalisation rather than controls that create a proper atmosphere for the growth of tourism. The entire world is our market. We cannot afford to overlook the capacity of tourism to generate employment. It the State's capacity is weak, new capacities can be created, as capacity is not destiny at all. We should also be able to take maximum advantage of the possibilities of tourism by consolidating or creating capacities.

Chapter 3

Model Law Regulating Activities of Travel Agencies, Tour Guides and Transferists: A Case Study of Macau

MACAU: A CASE STUDY

Decree-Law No. 48/98/M

November 3

CHAPTER I
GENERAL PROVISIONS

Article 1: Object

This law regulates the activity of travel agencies and the exercise of the professions of tour guide and of transferist.

Article 2: Concept

A travel agency, henceforth agency, is a commercial company registered in the Macau Special Administrative Region which is licensed in accordance with this law to exercise activities reserved to it.

Article 3: Reserved activities

1. The activities reserved to agencies are the following:
   (*a*) Procurement of travel documents, namely visas;

(*b*)   Organisation and sale of touristic trips;

(*c*)   Sale of tickets and reservation of seats in any means of transportation, as well as related luggage delivery;

(*d*)   Reservation of services in hotels and similar enterprises, as well as in any touristic enterprises;

(*e*)   Intermediation in the sale of services of similar agencies, whether local or from outside the Macau Special Administrative Region;

(*f*)   Reception, transfer and assistance to tourists.

2.   Agencies cannot refuse to render the services mentioned in subparagraphs: (*a*), (*c*) and (*d*) of the previous paragraph.

3.   The provision of touristic information is presumed to be conducted in the capacity of services intermediator, except when carried out by official entities acting within the scope of their functions, by transport enterprises or by organizers of conventions or exhibitions.

Article 4: Complementary Services

The following are services complementary to reserved activities of agencies:

(*a*)   Rental of vehicles, in accordance with the respective legislation;

(*b*)   Reservation and sale of tickets for shows and other public events;

(*c*)   Handling of insurance in authorized companies which underwrite risks arising from touristic activity;

(*d*)   Diffusion of touristic promotion materials, as well as the sale of touristic itineraries and similar publications;

(*e*)   (revoked).

Article 5: Forbidden Activities

1. If is forbidden for agencies to exercise any other activities or to render any other services besides the exercise of reserved activities or the rendering of complementary services allowed to them in accordance with this law.
2. It is forbidden for agencies to request or receive funds, patrimonial advantages or any other benefits from tour guides for the rendering of services in the framework of this law.

Article 6: Exclusivity

1. Only agencies can exercise reserved activities against remuneration.
2. The exercise of reserved activities is presumed to be against remuneration whenever carried out regularly or publicized under any title or in any manner.

Article 7: Activities Exercised by Other Entities

The provisions of articles 3 and 6 do not prevent the exercise of the following activities:

(*a*) The direct sale by hotels and similar enterprises, and by transport companies, of their services to clients;
(*b*) The transport of clients by hotels and similar enterprises with vehicles owned by them;
(*c*) The sale of services of a transport enterprise by other transport enterprise with which it has combined services;
(*d*) The making of reservation in hotels or similar enterprises by transport enterprises for users of their services.

Article 8: Prohibition to Refuse to Render Service

(revoked)

Article 9: Premises

1. Agencies must exercise their activity in autonomous premises, with independent acess, and which are exclusively for such exercise.
2. The activity of agencies shall be exercised in an immovable intended for commerce, services, offices or independent professions.
3. The premises shall have:
   (*a*) A minimum gross area of 40 square meters;
   (*b*) An area for serving clients;
   (*c*) Equipment appropriate to the exercise of their activities.
4. For the development of their activities, agencies may have branches and desks.
5. The provisions of paragraphs 1, 2 and 3 are applicable to branches, with the exception of subparagraph a) of paragraph 3; the minimum gross area of branches shall be 20 square meters.

Article 9-A: Compulsory Opening Hours

1. Agencies and their branches shall be open from 10:00 to 13:00 and from 15:00 to 18:00, except on Saturdays, Sundays and holidays, or in duly justified cases.
2. It is permitted to open outside the opening hours stated in the previous paragraph.
3. The provision of paragraph 1 is not applicable to desks.

Article 9-B: Identification of Vehicles

1. An identification tag shall be placed on vehicles used by agencies, in accordance with the model mentioned in annex IV to this law.
2. The tag shall include the designations of the agency, in a clearly visible manner.

Article 10: Designations

1. Only a company licensed to exercise the activity of travel agency may use such designation in its firm.

2. For the purpose of licensing, agencies may request to use a commercial fantasy name in addition to the firm mentioned in the previous paragraph, which shall remain common to the main enterprise, the branches and the desks.

3. The designations shall be compulsorily written in both official languages, without prejudice to the existence of a version in another language, namely in English.

4. There must be a certain degree of correspondence between the designations intended for use in the official languages.

5. For the purpose of licensing of the activity, only designations which cannot be confused with others of already existing agencies shall be approved, without prejudice to rights arising from industrial property.

6. An agency cannot use a designation other than that authorized, nor in any way allude to the previous one, in case the latter has been changed.

7. An agency must use in its external activity, namely in advertising, all authorized designations and, as well, the number of license given.

Article 11: Transfer of Ownership and Assignment of the Operation

1. The transfer of ownership and the assignment of the operation of an enterprise depend upon the transferee or assignee company holding a travel agency license.

2. The conclusion of any of the transactions mentioned in the previous paragraph shall be communicated, within 90 days, to the Macau Governement Tourist Office,

henceforth DST, by presenting the supporting documents.

Article 12: Diffusion and Information

1. Agencies shall promote the tourism of Macau by participating in events organised or supported by DST, and by displaying and distributing promotional materials and other documents sent by DST.

2. An agency must be able to supply updated information regarding the Macau Special Administrative Region concerning:

    (*a*) Means of transportation and of lodging;

    (*b*) Formalities relating to the arrival, stay and departure of tourists;

    (*c*) Exchange rates;

    (*d*) Regular touristic trips, if previously announced;

    (*e*) General touristic information.

3. Agencies must keep an updated record, which shall be accessible at all times, of:

    (*a*) Routes of touristic circuits in Macau, and the respective lists of tourists;

    (*b*) Tour guides, transferists and tour guide trainees for each excursion;

    (*c*) Vehicles of collective transportation used in each excursion;

    (*d*) Name of the responsible technical director.

Article 12-A: Internet

1. An agency's internet pages shall indicate in a clear and accurate manner the provision of subparagraph a) of paragraph 1 of article 41, and shall comply with the legislation on electronic commerce.

2. An agency shall communicate to DST, within thirty days, the creation of internet pages.

CHAPTER II
LICENSING PROCESS

Section I
License

Article 13: License

1. The exercise of the activity of agency depends upon a license to be granted by means of a dispatch of the Chief Executive.
2. The license is requested by means of an application presented to DST.

Article 14: Processing of Request

1. A request for a license to exercise the activity of agency shall mention:
   (a) Identification of the applicant company;
   (b) Location of the agency;
   (c) Denomination of the agency;
   (d) Complete identification of the agency's technical director.
2. The application shall have the following documents attached:
   (a) Certificate issued by the Commercial and Movable Property Registry relating to the registration of the applicant company;
   (b) Documents evidencing the fulfillment of the requirements relating to the agency's technical director;
   (c) Certificate issued by the Land Registry relating to the registration of the immovable to be used as premises of the agency, so as to show evidence in connection with the provision of paragraph 2 of article 9;

(*d*) Floor plan of the premises mentioned in the previous subparagraph, at a scale of 1:100.

3. Besides the documents mentioned in the previous paragraph, DST may request from the applicants, or from any other public entities or services, any other documents or elements that it deems necessary for better processing of the request.

4. The documents showing evidence of the bail and of the professional civil liability insurance mentioned in article 50 may the submitted after the approval of the request.

Article 15: Requirements

The issue of a license to exercise the activity of agency depends upon compliance by the applicant company with the following requirements:

(*a*) Incorporation by the applicant of a commercial company with registered office in Macau;

(*b*) Existence of a minimum registered company capital, fully paid, of an amount of $1,500,000,00 (one million and five hundred thousand patacas);

(*c*) Company object aiming exclusively at the operation of the activity of travel agency;

(*d*) Existence of at least one technical director;

(*e*) Provision of the guarantees required in Chapter VI, without prejudice to paragraph 4 of the previous article;

(*f*) Existence of premises in accordance with article 9.

Article 16: Opening of Branches and Desks

1. The issue by DST of a license to open branches depends upon the occurrence of all of the following requirements:

(*a*) Increase of the minimum registered company capital by at least $300,000,00 (three hundred thousand patacas) per branch;

    (*b*) Availability of appropriate premises in accordance with this law.

2. The opening of branches shall be preceded by an inspection to be conducted by DST.

3. It is permitted to open desks in the Macau International Airport, in maritime, road and rail terminals, and in border posts.

4. Besides the places mentioned in the previous paragraph, DST may authorize, in accordance with the circumstances, the opening of desks in other locations, namely in hotels.

Article 17: Branches — Processing of Request

1. A request for opening a branch shall mention:
    (*a*) Identification of the applicant company;
    (*b*) Location of the branch.

2. The application shall have the following documents enclosed:
    (*a*) Certificate issued by the Commercial and Movable Property Registry relating to the registration of the applicant company;
    (*b*) Certificate issued by the Land Registry relating to the registration of the immovable to be used as premises of the branch, so as to show evidence in connection with the provision of paragraph 2 of article 9;
    (*c*) Floor plan of the premises mentioned in the previous subparagraph, at a scale of 1:100.

Section II
License

Article 18: Issue

1. Once the exercise of the activity has been authorized, DST shall issue a license.

2. The issue of the license shall be preceded by an inspection of the premises, to be conducted by DST.

3. The license is issued in accordance with the model included as annex III to this law.

4. A fee is due for the issue of the license, in accordance with the table included as annex I to this law.

5. The license number is permanent, and is set sequencially in accordance with the date of the license issue.

Article 19: Validity

The license is valid for a period of one year, counted from the date of the first issue; the license is renewable.

Article 20: Renewal

1. The renovation of the license shall be applied for up to 30 days before the end of its validity period.

2. A fee is due for the renovation of the license, in accordance with the table included as annex I to this law.

3. If requested after the period mentioned in paragraph 1, the renovation of the license is subject to a supplementary fee stated in the table mentioned in the previous paragraph.

Article 21: Prior Authorization and Notice

1. After the issue of an agency's license, the following facts are subject to prior authorization by DST:

    (*a*) Changes to the agency's denomination;

    (*b*) Replacement of the technical director;

    (*c*) Opening of branches or desks.

2. An agency shall communicate to DST, by submitting the supporting documents, within ninety days from their occurrence:

(*a*)   Any changes to any element which is part of the request for a license to exercise the activity of agency;

(*b*)   Relocation of the main enterprise, of the branches or of the desks.

3.   A relocation of the main enterprise or of the branches requires an inspection of the new premises.

Article 22: Branches and Desks

1.   The number and location of the branches and desks must be specified in the license.

2.   Branches and desks can only be the object of a transaction which transfers their ownership, or assigns the right to operate them, if such is done together with the respective main enterprise.

Article 23: Publication of License

1.   DST shall arrange the publication of an extract of the license in the Official Bulletin; the respective expenses shall be borne by the interested party.

2.   For the purpose of the previous paragraph, an amount of no less than $1,000.00 (one thousand patacas) shall be handed together with the amount due for the issue of the license.

3.   Once the expenses have been calculated, any remaining balance in favour of the interested party shall be returned to him.

Article 23-A: Display of License

1.   A license issued in accordance with paragraph 3 of article 18 shall be displayed in a clearly visible place at the entrance of the main enterprise.

2.   Branches and desks must have a certified copy of the license, which shall be available for consultation by the entities mentioned in paragraph 1 of article

Section III
Lapse of License

Article 24: Lapse and Cancellation of License

1. An agency's license lapses and is cancelled whenever any of the following events occur:

    (*a*) The activity is not initiated within 90 days from its date of issue, except in cases of force majeure;

    (*b*) Bankruptcy, settlement with creditors, or termination of payments;

    (*c*) Termination of its activity;

    (*d*) Lack of application for renewal of the license for 2 consecutive years;

    (*e*) If any of the requirements mentioned in article 15 ceases to exist.

2. For the purpose of the effect mentioned in the previous paragraph, the lapse of the license shall be expressly recognized by DST.

3. An authorization for the opening of branches or desks shall lapse if they do not initiate operations within 90 days from the date of receipt of the respective notification, except in cases of force majeure.

Article 25: Termination of Payments

For the purpose of the previous article, it shall be deemed that termination of payments has occurred whenever the bail posted becomes insufficient for the payment of the debts recognized by the agency, and the agency neither pays the debts nor restores the bail in accordance with article 55.

Article 26: Termination of Activity

1. For the purpose of article 24, the closure of the enterprise for a period of time longer than 90 days without the presentation of an appropriate justification to DST shall

amount to a presumption that the agency has terminated its activity.

2. The presumption mentioned in the previous paragraph is applicable to branches and desks, with the necessary adaptations.

Article 27: Effect of Lapse of License

The lapse of the license and consequent cancellation shall cause the permanent closure of the agency, its branches and desks.

CHAPTER III
TECHNICAL DIRECTOR

Article 28: Requirements

1. Only persons who comply with the following requirements can be admitted as technical directors of agencies:

    (*a*) Residence in Macau;

    (*b*) Written and spoken knowledge of two languages, one of which shall be an official language;

    (*c*) Academic qualification at the level of a professional training course in the field of tourism, and recognized experience in the field.

2. For the purpose of subparagraph c) of the previous paragraph, the following situations shall be considered:

    (*a*) Professional training course offered or recognized in the Macau Special Administrative Region by an higher education institution specialized in the field of tourism;

    (*b*) Professional experience of no less than three years in activities in the tourism industry.

3. For the purpose of subparagraph b) of the previous paragraph, the applicant's résumé shall be assessed by a committee composed at least by two representatives of the Institute for Tourism Studies, henceforth IFT, and

one representative of DST, to be appointed by respective heads.

4. The committee shall express its opinion within 15 working days from the date of the application, after which it shall be deemed approved.

Article 29: Exclusivity

1. A person cannot hold simultaneously the position of technical director in more than one agency.

2. The presence of the technical director during the agency's opening hours is compulsory, except in duly justified cases.

Article 29-A: Substitution

1. In case of lack of a technical director due to force majeure, the agency shall propose within a maximum time limit of 15 days the hiring of a new technical director, in accordance with and for the purpose of subparagraph b) of paragraph 1 of article 21.

2. The failure to hire a technical director within 90 days from the date of the presentation of the last application, within the time limit specified in the previous paragraph, causes the suspension of the activity.

3. The suspension of the activity for more than 90 days causes the cancellation of the license.

Article 30: Evidence of Qualifications

1. Before taking up their positions, interested parties shall hand to DST the documents evidencing their academic qualifications and professional experience, for assessment of the requirements mentioned in article 28.

2. Besides the documents mentioned in the previous paragraph, DST may request from interested parties, or from any public departments or entities, other

elements deemed necessary for the purpose there mentioned.

3. The provisions of the previous paragraphs apply in case of substitution of the technical director.

CHAPTER IV
TOURISTIC TRIPS

Article 31: Concept

1. A touristic trip is any movement of persons within or to the outside of the Macau Special Administrative.
2. A touristic trip may be individual or collective.
3. Individual touristic trips are those agreed with a certain person or persons for the satisfaction of their interests or of programmes defined or accepted by them.
4. Collective touristic trips are those organised by agencies for groups of persons, by means of adherence to plans and prices globally and previously set.

Article 32: Excluded Activities

Those touristic trips where the agency merely acts as an intermediary in the sale or reservation of sporadic services specifically requested by the client shall not be deemed to be touristic trips.

Article 33: Insurance

Agencies organizing collective touristic trips are obliged to effect insurance covering the civil liability risks arising from such trips.

Article 34: Escort in Macau Collective Touristic Trips

It is compulsory to have escort by a tour guide in collective touristic trips, without prejudice to paragraph 1 of article 67-B.

Article 35: Excluded Trips

1. This law does not apply to collective trips within the Macau Special Administrative Region or to the outside, organised by:

    (*a*) Official entities acting within the scope of their functions;

    (*b*) Associations in which only the respective associates and their families take part, in accordance with their respective by-laws.

2. The exception mentioned in the previous paragraph depends upon the fulfillment of all of the following requirements:

    (*a*) Non-profit object;

    (*b*) Absence of commercial advertising, under any form or pretext.

CHAPTER V
RELATIONS WITH CLIENTS

Article 36: Liability

1. Agencies are liable towards their clients for the performance of the obligations arising from the sale of touristic trips, even if such obligations are to be executed by third parties, and without prejudice to the right of return, if applicable.

2. Agencies organizing touristic trips are jointly liable with the agencies selling such trips.

Article 37: Trip Programmes

1. Agencies organizing touristic trips shall have trip programmes to be handed to persons requesting them.

2. Such programmes shall accurately state the elements mentioned in subparagraphs (c) to (*h*) of paragraph 1 of article 41, and also:

(a) The existence of optional excursions, the respective price and the minimum number of participants, if applicable;

(b) The need for passport, visas and sanitary formalities for the requested trip and stay;

(c) The special conditions of the trip.

Article 38: Binding Effect of the Trip Programme

Agencies are bound to perform the trip programme, except if:

(a) The trip programme foresees the possibility of amendment of the conditions, and such amendment has been communicated to the client, in clear terms, prior to the conclusion of the contract;

(b) There is an agreement of the parties to the contrary.

Article 39: Obligation of Prior Information

Before the beginning of any trip, agencies shall provide to clients, with appropriate advance, in writing or in any other appropriate form, the following information:

(a) All clauses to be included in the contract;

(b) Timetables and places of stop and correspondence;

(c) How to make contact with the local representation of the agency or the entities which may assist the client should difficulties arise, or, in their absence, how to make contact with the agency itself;

(d) In cases of trips and stays of minors in foreign countries, how to directly contact those minors or the person locally responsible for their stay;

(e) The possibility to conclude an insurance contract covering the expenses arising from repatriation or assistance in case of accident or sickness;

(f) The need for travel documents, visas or any other formalities.

Article 40: Accessory Obligations

1. In the moment of sale of any service, agencies shall hand to clients a document mentioning the respective object and characteristics, the date of performance, the price and any payments already made.

2. When a trip exceeds 24 hours of duration or includes an overnight stay, agencies shall hand to the client a duly signed full copy of the contract.

3. Agencies shall provide to clients all elements necessary to obtain the service sold.

Article 41: Contract Contents

1. The sale of touristic trips requires the conclusion of a contract, which must mention the following:

    (*a*) Designations, address and license number of the agency selling and of the agency organizing the trip;

    (*b*) Insurance effected, if applicable;

    (*c*) Price of the trip organised, conditions and time limits in which its amendment is lawfully allowed, and any taxes or fees due for the trip which are not included in the price;

    (*d*) Amount or percentage of the price to be disbursed as initial payment, date of payment of the remaining amount, and consequences of the lack of payment;

    (*e*) Origin, itinerary and destination of the trip, periods and dates of stay;

    (*f*) Minimum number of participants required for helding the trip, and time limit for notification of cancellation to clients if such number is not reached;

    (*g*) Dates, times and places of departure and return, and categories and features of the means of transportation used;

(h) Type, rating and location of the accommodation used, with specification of meals included, if any;

(i) Visits, excursions or other services included in the price or paid optionally by the client;

(j) Conditions arising from special requests communicated by the client to the agency and accepted by the latter;

(k) Procedure for handling client complaints for non-performance of agreed services.

2. Without prejudice to paragraph 2 of the previous article, agencies shall hand to clients a document specifying clearly and inequivocally, even if in a simplified manner, the elements mentioned in the previous paragraph.

Article 42: Assistance to Clients

1. Whenever a client is not able to complete a trip as result of causes which are not imputable to him, the agency has the obligation to provide assistance to him up to the point of departure or destination, and shall adopt all measures necessary.

2. In case of complaints by clients, it is for the agency to produce evidence that it acted with diligence in order to find an adequate solution.

Article 43: Assignement of Contractual Position

1. A client may assign his position by replacing himself with another person who meets all the conditions required for the trip, provided that notice of the assignment is given to the agency three days in advance.

2. The assignor and the assignee are jointly liable for the payment of the price and of the additional expenses arising from the assignment.

Article 44: Impossibility to Perform

1. If it becomes impossible to fully perform the contract for causes not imputable to the agency, the agency must immediately inform the client of the causes of non-performance.

2. If the impossibility relates to an essential obligation, the client shall have the right to rescind the contract, in which case he shall communicate such intention to the agency in the shortest possible period of time.

Article 45: Change of Price by Agency

1. An agency can only change the price if all of the following requirements are met:

   (*a*) The contract expressly provides for such;

   (*b*) The change arises only from a variation in the cost of transportation or of fuel, of charges, taxes or fees payable, or from the fluctuation of exchange rates.

2. A change in the price which does not comply with the requirements mentioned in the previous paragraph grants to the client the right to rescind the contract in accordance with paragraph 2 of the previous article.

Article 46: Legal Effects of Rescission of Contract or Cancellation of Trip

1. If a client rescinds the contract in accordance with articles 44 or 45, or if the agency, as a result of facts not imputable to the client, cancels the touristic trip prior to the date of departure, the client, without prejudice to the civil liability of the agency, shall have the following rights:

   (*a*) To be refunded of all amounts paid; or

   (*b*) To choose to participate in another touristic trip, in which case the agency shall refund or the client shall pay any price difference.

2. There is no civil liability for the agency if the cancellation:

  (*a*) Is due to the fact that the number of participants in an organised trip is lower than the minimum number required, and the client has been informed of the cancellation in writing within the time limit foreseen;

  (*b*) Is not caused by overbooking;

  (*c*) Is caused by abnormal and unforeseeable circumstances, the results of which could not be avoided despite all measures adopted.

Article 47: Right of Rescission by Client

A client may rescind the contract at any time; however, he shall be liable for expenses already incurred by the agency, if justified, namely those arising from bookings effected that can no longer be cancelled.

Article 48: Non-performance

1. If, after departure, part of the services mentioned in the contract is not provided, the agency shall ensure, without price increases for the client, the provision of services equivalent to those agreed.

2. If the continuation of the trip becomes impossible, or if the conditions for continuation are not accepted by the client, the agency shall provide, without extra cost, an equivalent mean of transportation to enable the return to the departure point or to another agreed place.

3. In the cases mentioned in the previous paragraphs the client has the right to a refund of the difference between the price of the services agreed and that of those effectively provided, as well as the right to compensation in accordance with general rules.

Article 49: Liability for Goods Entrusted in Custody

An agency is liable for the loss, damage or disappearance of objects, money or luggage entrusted by the client to its custody.

CHAPTER VI
GUARANTEES

Section I
General Provisions

Article 50: Required Guarantees

1. In order to guarantee their liability towards the clients arising from the exercise of reserved activities, agencies are obliged to post a bail and to effect civil liability insurance.

2. Without prejudice to the provisions of general laws, the following namely are included in the scope of the previous paragraph:

    (*a*)   The refund of amounts paid by clients;

    (*b*)   The refund of supplementary expenses incurred by clients as a consequence of the non-performance of the services agreed or of their defective or insufficient performance;

    (*c*)   The compensation of patrimonial or personal damage caused to clients or to third parties by actions or ommissions of the agency or of its representatives;

    (*d*)   The repatriation of clients, and the provision of assistance to them, in accordance with article 42.

Article 51: Formalities

1. An agency cannot initiate or exercise its activity without producing evidence to DST that the guarantees required have been regularly contracted and are in force.

2. An agency must present annually to DST the documents evidencing that the bail and the insurance are in force.

Section II
Bail

Article 52: Bail

1. The guarantee arising from bail covers all acts practiced during its period of application.
2. In case of closure of an agency, regardless of the cause, the bail shall remain in force during the year following the closure, and is liable for all claims presented during that time period, provided that such claims arise from obligations contracted before closure.
3. For the purposes of this law, a closure shall be notified within 15 days to DST by means of a registered letter, and shall be verified by DST by means of an inspection.

Article 53: Amount

An agency shall post a bail of $500,000,00 (five hundred thousand patacas)

Article 54: Posting of Bail

Bail is posted by bank guarantee or deposit to the order of DST.

Article 55: Restoration

1. The bail shall be kept in force for the amount set.
2. If the bail is executed, the amount of coverage required must be restored.
3. For the purpose of the previous paragraph, DST shall notify the agency to restore the bail within 10 days.

4. Non-compliance with the previous paragraph causes the immediate temporary closure of the agency until the situation is regularized.

Article 56: Functioning

1. Payments for the account of the bail are made directly by the guarantor entity.
2. For the purpose of the previous paragraph, the client shall submit his request to DST, together with the documents evidencing his credit.
3. DST shall send to the guarantor entity its justified opinion on the request submitted by the client.

Article 57: Communication to DST

Guarantor entitities shall communicate to DST any payments effected under the bail, and any requests refused, indicating the grounds for refusal.

Section III
Professional Civil Liability Insurance

Article 58: Insurance

1. Insurance shall cover:
    (*a*) Personal, patrimonial and non-patrimonial damage caused to clients or to third parties by actions or omissions by the agency's legal representatives and the persons at its service and for which the agency has civil responsibility;
    (*b*) Supplementary expenses paid for by clients as a consequence of the nonperformance of services agreed or of their insuffient or defective performance.
2. Insurance does not cover:
    (*a*) Damage or harm caused to legal representatives of agencies and to persons at their service;

(*b*) Damage caused by the client or by third parties or arising from the nonperformance of legal rules in force relating to the services rendered by the agency or of instructions given by the agency.

3. Insurance may exclude damage or harm caused by accidents occurred with the means of transportation used in the services rendered by the agency, provided that these do not belong exclusively to the agency and that the transporter keeps in force the insurance required by the legal rules applicable to the means of transportation used.

4. If an agency organizes or proposes to organize touristic trips to foreign countries, insurance shall cover all countries visited.

Article 59: Amount

The insurance cover shall be of no less than $700,000,00 (seven hundred thousand patacas).

Article 60: Validity

Insurance shall be kept in force and updated.

Article 61: Restoration

If the insurance is rescinded or lapses as a result of a cause imputable to the agency, paragraphs 3 and 4 of article 55 shall apply, with the necessary adaptations.

CHAPTER VII
INSPECTION

Article 62: Competence

1. DST is empowered to:
   (*a*) Inspect compliance with this law;

(b) Process complaints presented;

(c) Instruct cases for breach of provisions of this law, and decide and apply the corresponding penalties.

2. If required to do so, administrative and police authorities shall provide assistance to DST officials in exercising their inspection function.

3. It is compulsory to provide any elements reasonably requested by duly identified officials on inspection duty.

Article 63: Report of Offences

All authorities and their officers shall communicate to DST any offences to this law.

CHAPTER VIII
TOUR GUIDE AND TRANSFERIST

Article 64: Concept and Qualifications of Guide

1. A tour guide is a professional which welcomes, informs and escorts tourists in Macau, against remuneration.

2. The exercise of the profession of tour guide depends upon:

(a) Residence in Macau; and

(b) Approval in a qualifying course offered by IFT; or

(c) Approval in a diploma or bachelor degree course in the field of tourism, offered by IFT or by other Macau higher education institution, or obtained in a higher education institution outside Macau, if accepted by IFT;

(d) Registration in DST and issuance of a tour guide card, in accordance with the model included as annex II to this law;

(e) Contractual link with a travel agency.

3. Persons qualified under the terms and conditions mentioned in subparagraph c) of the previous paragraph can only exercise the profession and obtain the respective registration and tour guide card after attending a seminar and obtaining approval in an exam mentioned in paragraph 1 of article 67.

Article 65: Course to be Offered by IFT

(revoked).

Article 66: Identification of Guide

1. The tour guide card must be compulsorily used, and it shall be worn in a manner that enables the easy identification of its holder and of the agency with which he has a contractual link.
2. The identification of the agency shall be mentioned in a label affixed to the tour guide card, in accordance with the model included as annex II to this law.
3. (revoked).
4. (revoked).

Article 67: Tour Guide Card

1. The tour guide card, as well as its registration, shall lapse within three years if its holder, during that period, does not attend any of the seminars mentioned in article 67-E or, in case he attends them, if he fails to obtain approval in a final exam.
2. The renewal of the tour guide card is done every three years, upon application of the interested party, presented together with a certificate issued by IFT evidencing the attendance of the seminar and the approval in the final exam mentioned in the previous paragraph.
3. (revoked).

Article 67-A: Tour Guide Trainee

1. Students who attend or obtain approval in the courses mentioned in paragraph 2 of article 64 are tour guide trainees.

2. The escort of a touristic trip by a tour guide trainee shall be conducted in the dependence of a fully certified guide.

3. The identification card, as per the model included as annex II to this law, is of compulsory use, and it shall be worn in a manner that enables an easy identification of its holder and of the agency for which he works.

4. The card mentioned in the previous paragraph is issued by DST upon application of the agency.

Article 67-B: Concept and Qualifications of Transferist

1. A transferist is a professional hired by an agency who welcomes and escorts tourists between border posts and between these and the hotels, against remuneration.

2. The exercise of the profession of transferist depends upon the conclusion of general secondary school, the attendance of a seminar especially organised for this purpose by IFT, after having consulted DST, and the approval on the respective final exam.

3. A transferist qualified in accordance with the previous paragraph is only authorized to exercise the profession after registration with DST and the issuance of a transferist card, in accordance with the model included as annex II to this law.

Article 67-C: Identification of Transferist

It is compulsory to wear the card, and it shall be worn so as to enable the easy identification of its holder and of the agency that hired him.

Article 67-D: Transferist Card

1. The issue or renewal of the card depends upon an application of the contracting agency, which shall be accompanied by a certificate issued by IFT evidencing attendance of the seminar and approval in the exam mentioned in paragraph 2 of article 67-B.

2. The renewal of the card is done every three years, in accordance with the previous paragraph.

3. The transferist card lapses in case of rescission or lapse of the contract with the agency.

4. The agency shall communicate to DST the facts mentioned in the previous paragraph, within no more than 15 days from their occurrence.

Article 67-E: Knowledge Update

1. IFT shall annually organize knowledge update seminars for tour guides and transferists on matters in the fields of tourism, culture and economy.

2. The subject of the seminars and the specific topics of the respective exams shall be submitted to DST for prior approval.

3. The opening of a seminar shall be preceded by the publication of a notice in at least two of the local dailies of larger circulation, one in Chinese language and the other in Portuguese language.

Article 68: Professional Codes of Conduct

1. In providing information to tourists, tour guides and transferists must strictly abey by the truth.

2. In exercising their functions, tour guides and transferists must not:

    (*a*) Induce tourists to effect purchases in certain and determined enterprises;

(b)   Request or receive money, patrimonial advantages or any other benefit from another guide for the provision of services in the framework of this law;

(c)   Participate in any kind of game of fortune;

(d)   Promote and market goods.

Article 69: Inspection

1.   DST, police authorities and their officers have competence to inspect compliance with the provisions of this law.

2.   Offences detected by police authorities and their officers shall be mentioned in an offence report which shall be sent to DST.

Article 69-A: Offence Report

1.   The offence report shall state the identification of the agency, the guide or the transferist, depending on the case, the place, day and time of the occurrence of the offence, the circumstances in which it has been committed, a specified account of the offence with reference to the legal provisions violated, and any other elements deemed useful.

2.   The offence report shall also be signed by a representative of the agency, by the guide or by the transferist, as alleged offenders, depending on the case, therein mentioning expressly, if that is the case, any refusal to sign.

3.   A single report may mention all offences committed in a single occasion or related to one another, even if the offenders are different.

4.   Once a report has been received, a case officer shall be appointed.

CHAPTER IX
RULES ON OFFENCES

Section I
Offences in General

Article 70: Enumeration

Breaches of this law shall be punished with the following penalties:

- (*a*) Warning;
- (*b*) Fine;
- (*c*) Temporary closure of the enterprise;
- (*d*) Permanent closure of the enterprise and cancellation of the licence;
- (*e*) Cancellation of the tour guide card;
- (*f*) Cancellation of the transferist card.

Article 71: Repeat Offences

1. For the purpose of this law, there is a repeat offense whenever another offense of the same type is committed within 1 year from a final conviction.
2. In case of repeat offences, the amount of the fine shall be the double of that previously applied or, if other penalty was applied, the next more serious penalty shall be applied.

Article 72: Succession

A succession of offences is an aggravating circumstance, irrespective of the time period in which they occurred or of the respective nature.

Article 73: Payment of Fine

1. If a fine is applied, the offender shall voluntarily effect payment within ten days from the date of notification of the dispatch that applied the penalty.

2. In the absence of voluntary payment of the fine, forced execution shall be resorted to in accordance with the procedure for the execution of tax debts, through the competent authority; a certificate of the dispatch that applied the penalty shall serve as executive title.

Article 74: Accumulation of Liability

The application of any of the penalties mentioned in article 70 is separate from civil or criminal liability as may occur in the case.

Article 75: Limits and Criteria

The penalties shall be set within the limits mentioned in this law, taking into account:

(*a*) The nature and circumstances of the offence;
(*b*) The harm caused to clients, to third parties and to the image of the tourism of the Macau Special Adminstrative Region;
(*c*) The repeat offender status of the agency.

Article 76: Publicity

Whenever the seriousness or the circumstances of an offense in a particular case so warrant, the penalty applied may be publicized through the media.

Article 77: Appeal

(revoked).

Section II
Offenses

Article 78: Illegal Exercise of Activity

1. The exercise of the activity of agency without a license issued in accordance with this law shall be punished

with the immediate closure and a fine of $120,000,00 (one hundred and twenty thousand patacas).

2. For the purpose of the previous paragraph, DST may use police authorities to enforce the closure.

Article 79: Illegal Opening of Branch or Desk

A breach of article 16 shall be punished with the permanent closure of the branch or desk and a fine of $20,000,00 (twenty thousand patacas) for each offence.

Article 80: Transfer of Branch or Desk

A breach of paragraph 2 of article 22 shall be punished with the permanent closure of the branch or desk and a fine of $10,000,00 (ten thousand patacas), for each offence.

Article 81: Lack of Technical Director

1. The operation of an agency without a technical director shall be punished with a fine of $20,000,00 (twenty thousand patacas).
2. Without prejudice to the previous paragraph, the agency must engage a technical director in accordance with the provisions of this law.
3. Non-compliance with the previous paragraph causes the suspension of the agency's activity.
4. A suspension of the activity for more than 90 days causes the cancellation of the license.

Article 82: Irregular Touristic Trips

A breach of paragraph 2 of article 35 causes:

(*a*) A report, for disciplinary purposes, to the supervisor of the entity organizing the trip;
(*b*) The application to the association responsible for the trip of a fine of $5,000,00 (five thousand patacas) to $10,000,00 (ten thousand patacas).

Article 82-A: Unescorted Collective Touristic Trips

A breach of article 34 shall be punished with a fine of $40,000,00 (forty thousand patacas) to $60,000,00 (sixty thousand patacas).

Article 83: Illegal Exercise of Professions of Tour Guide and Transferist

1. A breach of paragraph 2 of article 64 and of paragraph 3 of article 67-B shall be punished with a fine of $20,000,00 (twenty thousand patacas) to $30,000,00 (thirty thousand patacas), applicable to the offender.
2. The agency shall be punished with the double of the fine applied to the offender.

Article 84: Non-compliance with Time Limit

(revoked).

Article 85: Unauthorized Actions

1. A breach of paragraph 2 of article 68 shall be punished with a fine of $20,000,00 (twenty thousand patacas) to $30,000,00 (thirty thousand patacas), applicable to the offender.
2. Paragraph 2 of article 83 shall apply to this offense.

Article 86: Non-renewal of Card

(revoked).

Article 87: Wrong Information

1. The provision by tour guides, transferists or agencies of information which grossly distorts factual realities shall be punished with a fine of $5,000,00 (five thousand patacas) to $10,000,00 (ten thousand patacas), applicable

to the offender, provided that all of the following requirements are met:

(*a*) Taking their functions into account, the knowledge of such facts can be legally required from them;

(*b*) The correct clarification of such facts is inherent to the normal exercise of their functions; and

(*c*) The provision of such information is likely to cause considerable damage to the client, or is made with the intention to obtain an illegitimate benefit, to himself or to a third party.

2. If the fact mentioned in the previous paragraph, although commited by the guide or transferist, is imputable to an act or omission of the agency, the latter shall be punished with a fine within the limits therein set.

Article 88: Breach of Duty to Render Assistance

A refusal to perform the duty to render assistance stated in article 42 shall be punished with a fine of $5,000,00 (five thousand patacas) to $10,000,00 (ten thousand patacas).

Article 88-A: Various Offences

1. A breach of paragraph 2 of article 5, of article 9, of article 9-B, of paragraph 1 of article 29, of article 29-A, and of article 33, shall be punished with a fine of $10,000,00 (ten thousand patacas) to $20,000,00 (twenty thousand patacas).

2. A breach of paragraph 2 of article 3, of paragraph 1 of article 5, of article 12, of paragraph 2 of article 29, of subparagraphs b) to e) of article 39, of paragraphs 1 and 2 of article 40, of article 41, of paragraphs 1 and 2 of article 48 and of paragraph 4 of article 67-D shall be punished with a fine of $5,000,00 (five thousand patacas) a $10,000,00 (ten thousand patacas).

3. A breach of paragraph 1 of article 9-A, of paragraphs 6 and 7 of article 10, of paragraph 2 of article 11, of article 12-A, of paragraphs 1 and 2 of article 21, of article 23-A, of article 37, of subparagraphs a) and f) of article 39, of paragraph 3 of article 40, of paragraph 1 of article 44, of paragraphs 1 and 2 of article 66, of paragraph 3 of article 67-A, of article 67-C, and of paragraph 1 of article 103, shall be punished with a fine of $1,000,00 (one thousand patacas) to $5,000,00 (five thousand patacas).

4. A breach of paragraph 3 of article 12 shall be punished with a fine of $20,000,00 (twenty thousand patacas).

Article 89: Repeat Offences

1. The practice of repeated and serious offences by a travel agency causes the permanent closure of the agency, its branches and desks, without prejudice to the application of penalties arising from each offence.

2. The practice of repeated offences by a tour guide or transferist causes the cancellation of his card, without prejudice to the application of penalties regarding each offence.

3. The cancellation of the card causes, as well, the loss of the right to request the issue of a new card, for a period of one year.

CHAPTER X
PROCEDURE

Article 90: Offence Report

(revoked).

Article 91: Investigation

(revoked).

Global Tourism Policies, Laws, Action Plans

Article 92: Report

(revoked).

Article 93: Acusation

(revoked).

Article 94: Procedure

(revoked).

CHAPTER XI
FINAL AND TEMPORARY PROVISIONS

Article 95: Designation

(revoked).

Article 96: Scope of Application

(revoked).

Article 97: Update of Guarantees

(revoked).

Article 98: Register

1. DST shall organize and keep updated a register of:
    (*a*) Agencies, branches and desks;
    (*b*) Technical directors;
    (*c*) Tour guides;
    (*d*) Transferists;
    (*e*) Tour guide trainees.
2. The register may be consulted by interested parties, including agencies or other entities providing services in the field of tourism.

Article 99: Lapse of Authorizations

(revoked).

Article 100: Fees

Fees are due for conducting inspections, in accordance with the table included as annex I to this law.

Article 101: Destination of Fees and Expenses

The amounts arising from fees and expenses mentioned in this law, as well as from fines applied, shall be income of the Macau Tourism Fund.

Article 102: Tour Guides

(revoked).

Article 103: Statistic Information

1. Agencies are obliged to send quarterly to DST quantitative information on individual or collective trips performed with their intermediation within or to the outside of Macau during that period, indicating the nationalities of the travellers and the countries or territories of origin or destination.
2. The previous paragraph does not affect the information that must be provided by agencies to Statistics and Census Service for statistic purposes.

Article 104: Revocation

Decree-Law no. 25/93/M, of May 31, and Portaria no. 163/93/M, of May 31, are revoked.

Article 105: Start of Application

This law shall start to apply 30 days from the date of its publication.

Annexure
TABLE OF EXPENSES AND FEES

1. Conduction of inspection $500,00
2. Issue of license $25,000,00
3. Renovation of license $5,000,00
4. Addicional fee for late renewal of license
   (a) Up to thirty days $1,000,00
   (b) More than thirty days $5,000,00
5. First issue of identification card $100,00
6. Second issue of identification card $200,00
7. Other issuances $500,00
8. Renewal of identification card $100,00
9. Addicional fee for late renewal of identification card
   (a) Up to thirty days $100,00
   (b) More than thirty days $200,00

Chapter 4

Model Laws, Policies and Action Plans Concerning Sex Tourism of Children Worldwide

MODEL LAWS CONCERNING SEX TOURISM OF CHILDREN

United States Policy

The United States has established laws that make it illegal to travel to another country with the intent to engage in sex with minors.

18 U.S.C. 2423B—Travel with Intent to Engage in Sexual Acts with a Juvenile: A person who travels in interstate commerce, or conspires to do so, or a citizen of the United States or an alien admitted for permanent residence in the United States who travels in foreign commerce, or conspires to do so, for the purpose of engaging in a sexual act with a person [younger than] 18 years of age that would be in violation of Chapter 109A if the sexual act occurred in the special maritime and territorial jurisdiction of the United States shall be fined under this title, imprisoned not more than 10 years, or both.

International Cooperation

The sex tourism industry has no territorial boundaries; therefore, in order to successfully combat this problem when

re victimized, it must be viewed from an international
ve. To stop sex tourism of children, effective laws and
forcement is vital. Many countries have passed new
es or are considering amendments to their national laws
to address the commercial-sexual exploitation of children and
hold offenders accountable. Several destination countries have
recently strengthened their laws addressing the prostitution of
children in an effort to stem the influx of sex tourists and protect
their children from exploitation. The Philippine government
has increased the attention on foreign "child-sex tourists" and
promoted the Special Protection of Children Against Child
Abuse, Exploitation and Discrimination Act. The Act creates
criminal offenses aimed at patrons, procurers, advertisers,
pimps, and brothel owners. Another section of this Act provides
that convicted foreigners will be deported and banned from
returning, but only after serving their sentences. Further, the
Czech Republic now provides for prosecution of those who
traffic in children.

The responsibility for curbing sex tourism of children cannot
rest solely with the destination countries. Sending countries
must also act to punish those who travel to sexually exploit
children. More recent efforts, turned to holding these sex tourists
accountable in their home countries. The Criminal Code of
Germany was amended in 1993 to allow prosecution of
Germans who travel for this purpose, regardless of where the
act occurs. Australia's Crimes (Child-Sex Tourism) Amendment
Act 1994 criminalizes 'sexual intercourse with someone who is
younger than 16 years of age while outside of Australia and
applies to Australian citizens or residents of Australia. Countries
that have tightened their national laws against sex tourism of
children have taken different approaches some of which could
be used as examples. Combining these approaches could also
result in a comprehensive statute encompassing all potential
activities supporting the sexual exploitation of children through
prostitution.

There are also transitional and international governing
bodies that help combat the commercial sexual exploitation of
children. In recent years several international conferences have

been held involving governments as well as nongovernmental organisations to handle sex tourism of children as an international community. One of which is the World Congress Against Commercial Sexual Exploitation of Children. Another is the United Nations' Convention on the Rights of a Child which is a fundamental and important document as excerpted below.

The United Nations Convention on the Rights of the Child

The Convention on the Rights of the Child was carefully drafted over the course of 10 years (1979-1989) with the input of representatives from all societies, all religions, and all cultures. On November 20, 1989, the General Assembly of the United Nations unanimously adopted the Convention on the Rights of the Child. This is probably the most significant of all international instruments because many of the signatory countries base their legislation against child sexual exploitation on this document. The Convention expressly condemns the sexual exploitation of minors in prostitution and illegal sexual practices.

The member states of the United Nations, convinced that the exploitation of children is a paramount concern, set forth to establish procedures that protected children against continuing and evolving violations to their rights.

The Convention

The Convention consists of 54 Articles, all regarding the rights of a child. The excerpts noted below are Articles from the Convention directly related to the sexual exploitation of children.

Article 1

For the purposes of the present Convention, a child means every human being [younger than] 18 years unless, under the law applicable to the child, majority is attained earlier.

Article 19

1. States Parties shall take all appropriate legislative, administrative, social, and educational measures to protect the child from all forms of physical or mental violence, injury, abuse, neglect or negligent treatment, maltreatment or exploitation, including sexual abuse, while in the care of parent(s), legal guardian(s), or any other person who has the care of the child.

2. Such protective measures should, as appropriate, include effective procedures for the establishment of social programmes to provide necessary support for the child and for those who have the care of the child, as well as for other forms of prevention and for identification, reporting, referral, investigation, treatment, and follow-up of instances of child maltreatment described heretofore, and, as appropriate, for judicial involvement.

Article 34

States Parties undertake to protect the child from all forms of sexual exploitation and sexual abuse. For these purposes, States Parties shall in particular take all appropriate national, bilateral, and multilateral measures to prevent

(*a*) The inducement or coercion of a child to engage in any unlawful sexual activity;

(*b*) The exploitative use of children in prostitution or other unlawful sexual practices;

(*c*) The exploitative use of children in pornographic performances and materials

Article 35

Obligates states to prevent the abduction, sale, and trafficking of children.

Implementation of the Convention

The Convention reflects a global consensus and, in a very short period of time, it has become the most widely accepted human rights treaty ever. As of 2002, it has been ratified by 191 countries; only three countries have not ratified. The United States, which has signaled its intention to ratify by formally signing the Convention, now stands as the only industrialized country in the world and one of only two United Nations member States yet to make this legal commitment to children. The other country is Somalia, which is presently without a recognized government. Timor-Leste, which became independent in May 2002, also has yet to ratify the Convention.

As in many other nations, the United States undertakes an extensive examination and scrutiny of treaties before proceeding to ratify. This examination, which includes an evaluation of the degree of compliance with existing law and practice in the country at state and federal levels, can take several years—or even longer if the treaty is portrayed as being controversial or if the process is politicized.

The United Nations Convention on the Rights of the Child established a Committee on the Rights of the Child for the purpose of monitoring the progress of parties. Signatory states are required to file a report to the Committee on the Rights of the Child within two years of when they ratified it, from that point they must file a report every five years. Under the Convention, nongovernment organisations (NGOs) from signatory states are also encouraged to file reports declaring the status of children in their country, as it relates to the Convention.

World Congress Against Commercial Sexual Exploitation of Children

In 1996 the First World Congress Against Commercial Sexual Exploitation of Children was convened in Stockholm, Sweden, as a forum to develop strategies for an international response. The World Congress adopted a Declaration and Agenda for

Action that highlights existing international commitments, identifies priorities for action, and assists in the implementation of relevant international instruments. It calls for action from governments; all sectors of society; and national, regional, and international organisations against the commercial-sexual exploitation of children. It emphasizes cooperation, prevention, and protection of children; recovery; and rehabilitation. In addition it promotes the participation of children in developing and implementing governmental programmes designed to help them.

In December 2001 the Second World Congress on Commercial Sexual Exploitation of Children, hosted by the Japanese Government in association with the Prefecture of Yokohama, took place in Yokohama. In attendance were representatives of 35 states who did not participate in the first Congress, the number of states committed under the Agenda for Action now totals 159.

The objectives of the Second World Congress were to enhance political commitment to the implementation of the Agenda for Action adopted at the First World Congress; review progress in the implementation of this Agenda; share expertise and good practices; identify main problem areas and/or gaps in the fight against commercial sexual exploitation of children; strengthen the follow-up process of the World Congress.

WTO STATEMENT ON THE PREVENTION OF ORGANIZED SEX TOURISM

Whereas the WTO Tourism Bill of Rights and Tourist Code (Sofia, 1985) calls on States and individuals to prevent any possibility of using tourism to exploit others for prostitution purposes.

Having consulted international and national organizations concerned, both governmental and non-governmental, as well as the representatives of the tourism sector.

Considering the preoccupation of the international community over the persistence of organized sex tourism which, for the purpose of this statement, can be defined as "trips organized from within the tourism sector, or from outside this sector but using its structures and networks, with the primary purpose of effecting a commercial sexual relationship by the tourist with residents at the destination".

Aware of the grave health as well as social and cultural consequences of this activity for both tourist receiving and sending countries, especially when it exploits gender, age, social and economic inequality at the destination visited.

The General Assembly

Rejects all such activity as exploitative and subversive to the fundamental objectives of tourism in promoting peace, human rights, mutual understanding, respect for all peoples and cultures, and sustainable development.

Denounces and condemns in particular child sex tourism, considering it a violation of Article 34 of the Convention on the Rights of the Child (United Nations, 1989), and requiring strict legal action by tourist sending and receiving countries.

Requests governments of both tourist sending and receiving countries to Mobilize their competent departments, including National Tourism Administrations, to undertake measures against organized sex tourism.

Gather evidence of organized sex tourism and encourage education of concerned government officials and top executives in the tourism sector about the negative consequences of this activity.

Issue guidelines to the tourism sector insisting that it refrains from organizing any forms of sex tourism, and from exploiting prostitution as a tourist attraction.

Establish and enforce, where applicable, legal and administrative measures to prevent and eradicate child sex tourism, in particular through bilateral agreements to facilitate, inter alia, the prosecution of tourists engaged in any unlawful sexual activity involving children and juveniles.

Assist intergovernmental and non-governmental organizations concerned in taking action against organized forms of sex tourism.

Appeals to donor countries, aid agencies and other sources of finance to engage in tourism development projects seeking to enhance and diversify the supply of tourism services at the destinations affected by sex tourism, so as to foster employment opportunities in the tourism sector, develop its linkages with other sectors of the national economy, and contribute to tourism's social and economic sustainability.

Commends the tourism companies and tourism industry organizations, as well as non-governmental organizations such as ECPAT, which have already undertaken measures against sex tourism, in particular with respect to the sexual exploitation of children and juveniles.

Appeals to the travel trade to:

1. Join efforts and cooperate with non-governmental organizations to eliminate organized sex tourism, at both the origin and destination of travel flows, by identifying and focusing on the critical points at which this activity can proliferate;

2. Educate staff about the negative consequences of sex tourism, including its impact on the image of the tourism sector and tourist destinations, and invite staff to find ways to remove commercial sex services from the tourism offer;

3. Develop and strengthen professional codes of conduct and industry self-regulatory mechanisms against the practice of sex tourism;

4. Adopt practical, promotional and commercial measures, such as, for example, positive self-identification of enterprises which refrain from engaging in sex tourism; banning commercial sex services, in particular involving children, on the contracted tourism premises; providing information to travellers about health risks of sex tourism, etc.;

5. Warn tourists particularly against engaging in child sex tourism, denouncing its criminal nature and the manner in which children are forced into prostitution;

6. Encourage the media to assist the tourism sector in its action to uncover, isolate, condemn and prevent all organized forms of sex tourism;

7. Invites countries and their tourism entities to contribute to the World Congress on the Commercial Sexual Exploitation of Children, organized jointly by the Swedish Government and UNICEF, to be held in Stockholm, Sweden, in August 1996.

IFWTO (INTERNATIONAL FEDERATION OF WOMEN'S TRAVEL ORGANIZATIONS)

Resolution Against Sex Tourism

Whereas, The IFWTO dedicated to improving the status of women in the travel industry and promoting international goodwill and understanding recognizes that "sex tourism" is a growing problem affecting both industrialized and developing countries, and

Whereas, The IFWTO, in full cooperation with the World Tourism Organization, industry associations, governments and non-governmental organizations condemns "sex tourism", and encourages members and associations to work within the legal, ethical, and cultural limits of their country against all aspects of organized "sex tourism"; and

Whereas, That recognizing the physical, social, and mental damage caused by "sex tourism", IFWTO members and associates pledge to support local, regional and international campaigns or organizations to help restore the rights, dignity and health of victims of "sex tourism"; therefore be it

Resolved, That as responsible tourism professionals, IFWTO members and associates pledge to exercise vigilance in respect to the activities of their customers when brought to their attention. They will act in accordance with the legislation of the countries involved, and within the dictates of their own conscience; and

Resolved, That IFWTO members and associates pledge to combat the prostitution of women and children related to organized "sex tourism" and to protect the victims of such tourists by:

- Supporting the measures taken by governments to counter the sexual exploitation of women and children,
- Informing colleagues of the negative consequences of "sex tourism",
- Advising clients of the penalties imposed on tourists who commit acts involving the use of children for the purposes of sexual gratification.

Resolved, That IFWTO members and associates pledge never to promote or assist in the promotion of travel, tours or Programmes designed for sexual exploitation and to encourage local, regional and national measures to prevent and eradicate "sex tourism".

CHILD PROTECTION

North American Travel Industry Joins UNICEF in the Fight Against Child Exploitation

Her Majesty, Queen Sylvia of Sweden, reaffirmed her commitment to the fight to protect children from sexual predators today during a conference on how to protect children from sexual exploitation organized by UNICEF. The conference marked the launch of a "Code of Conduct" for the North American travel industry, which was signed by Carlson Company Inc's Chairman Marilyn Carlson Nelson.

Queen Sylvia called the sexual exploitation of children a "serious and unacceptable crime against humanity."

The code is designed to protect children from commercial sexual exploitation, a multi-billion dollar industry in which as many as 2 million children are sexually exploited each year.

A high-level panel of experts spoke at a panel at UNICEF headquarters during the conference, including:

- Dawid de Villiers of the World Tourism Organization (WTO);
- John Miller from the U.S. State Department;
- Carol Smolenski from ECPAT (End Child Prostitution, Child Pornography and the Trafficking of Children for Sexual Purposes) USA; and
- UNICEF Executive Director Carol Bellamy.

"The travel industry is critical in the fight against commercial sexual exploitation," said Ms. Bellamy. "We can no longer look the other way while members of our own communities are abusing children in the most unthinkable ways. These are perpetrators of the worst kind. They not only display a callous disregard for human dignity, they do so with total impunity."

The Code of Conduct Protect Children Everywhere

UNICEF joined the World Tourism Organization and the international advocacy group ECPAT in launching the Code of Conduct.

Queen Sylvia hosted the first World Congress on Commercial Exploitation of Children in 1996 in Stockholm, Sweden. The Code of Conduct was initiated in April 1998 by ECPAT Sweden in cooperation with the Scandinavian Tourism Industry and the World Tourism Organization.

The Code is a voluntary procedure, currently implemented in 45 countries around the world. By signing the Code, the hotel and travel industry (including travel agents, airlines, hotel workers, etc) commit themselves to halting the sexual exploitation of children by various means, including:

- Establishing an ethical corporate policy against commercial sexual exploitation of children;
- Training personnel in the country where children are sexually exploited;
- Introducing clauses in contracts with suppliers, stating a common repudiation of sexual exploitation of children; and
- Providing information on the sexual exploitation of children to travellers.

Combating Commercial Sex Tourism

The launch of the North American "Code of Conduct" is a necessary tool for the travel industry to combat the sinister and often hidden world of commercial sex tourism involving sex with minors (according to the Convention on the Rights of the Child, any boy or girl under the age of eighteen is considered a minor).

"It is everyone's responsibility to protect children from commercial sexual exploitation," said Carol Smolenski, Director of ECPAT USA. "The code is a perfect example of how the travel industry can do its part in building a protective environment for children."

According to UNICEF, at the end of 2000, as many as 325,000 children were at risk of commercial sexual exploitation in the United States alone. According to ECPAT USA, an estimated 25 per cent of sex tourists outside the United States are American.

To combat this growing problem, laws are being passed in many countries, including the United States, which make it illegal to travel overseas to engage in sexual acts with a minor.

After signing the code, Ms. Carlson Nelson urged her competitors in the travel industry to get involved in the fight to protect children from sex tourists.

COMBATING CHILD SEX TOURISM

The expansion of tourism over the past half-century has more recently been accompanied by an increase in child sex tourism.

The main perpetrators of child sexual exploitation in tourism are not 'real' paedophiles but people who take advantage of being in another country to ignore the social taboos which would normally govern their behaviour ("preferential abusers" and "occasional abusers"). The World Congress against Commercial Sexual Exploitation of Children, held in Stockholm in August 1996, provided an opportunity to define this phenomenon more clearly.

The Commission is concerned about the increase in child sexual exploitation and the fact that it is spreading geographically, and wants the Member States and the tourism industry to become more closely involved in fighting this scourge. To this end, it intends to encourage the drawing-up and implementation of codes of conduct which are in line with the tourism ethic as laid down in the Tourism Bill of Rights and the Tourist Code adopted by the World Tourism Organisation in 1985.

Practical steps have already been taken, including the measures referred to in the Communication on harmful and illegal content on the Internet, the Green Paper on the protection of minors and human dignity in audiovisual and information services (October 1996), and the Communication on trafficking in women for the purpose of sexual exploitation (November 1996).

In practical terms, the Commission is considering EU measures in three priority areas:

Deterring and Punishing Child Sex Abusers

It is important to get rid of any legal vacuums that may exist, in particular by enacting laws to punish offenders for offences and crimes committed against children abroad, and by giving national courts extra-territorial jurisdiction in this area, even where the presumed offence or crime is not provided for under the laws of the country in which it was committed. It is clear from initial assessments that increased judicial cooperation between the Member States is needed.

The collection and exchange of information on the social aspects of sex tourism will improve understanding of this phenomenon. For example, such information could cover the links between tourism and prostitution, the identity, motivation and behaviour of sex tourists, and the public health implications of sex tourism.

Preventive measures could be taken by the national tourism authorities, particularly by providing information for travellers. As well as making them aware of differences between the foreign country and their own, travellers would be reminded of the need to respect the values of the country being visited and to comply with certain basic rules of behaviour. A coordinated EU response could then be considered by the Advisory Committee in the field of tourism, made up of members designated by each Member State, and at the Commission's consultation meetings with the tourism industry.

Stemming the Flow of Sex Tourists from the Member States

The reasons underlying the supply side of child sex tourism are as numerous as they are complex, although poverty is one of the main factors. The Commission intends to focus its action primarily on the demand side because child sex tourists come mainly from industrialised countries, including EU Member States.

To this end, coordinated public information and awareness-raising campaigns against child sex tourism could be organised. The Community would provide funding for these campaigns and would mobilise the various Community information networks. Programmes and training modules for people working in the tourism industry (including students being trained in the tourism sector) could give them guidelines for combating child sex tourism. Finally, the drafting and tightening-up of codes of conduct and self-regulatory mechanisms in the tourism industry would be important instruments. The Commission will push for the various branches of the tourism industry to sign up to a basic minimum set of commitments.

Helping to Combat Sex Tourism in Third Countries

This line of action is in keeping with the principle of respect for human rights both within and outside the Union, as laid down in the treaties and agreements the EU has concluded with countries outside the Union. While the sexual exploitation of children for commercial purposes is not actually perpetrated by governments, the Commission will apply pressure on countries which appear to be dilatory in this regard.

With regard to financing, the Commission will act in accordance with the principles of rationalising methods for action and coordinating the Community resources available for the protection of children who are victims of sex tourism. Existing instruments for promoting and protecting the rights of the child could be used specifically to support measures to help children who are victims of sex tourism. At the same time, there should be political dialogue with the developing countries most affected. Other measures could be considered once a more detailed analysis has been undertaken of the nature and extent of child sex tourism and of the measures implemented by the countries concerned.

Conclusion

The EU Member States have a duty to take practical steps to combat child sex tourism:

- In view of the countries of origin of the tourists involved;
- To prevent the development of child prostitution in Europe; and
- Because they have ratified the Convention on the rights of the child.

The Facts About Child Sex Tourism

There's a special evil in the abuse and exploitation of the most innocent and vulnerable. The victims of sex trade see little of life before they see the very worst of life—an underground of brutality and lonely fear.

—*George W. Bush*

What is Child Sex Tourism?

Each year over a million children are exploited in the global commercial sex trade. Child sex tourism (CST) involves people who travel from their own country to another and engage in commercial sex acts with children. CST is a shameful assault on the dignity of children and a form of violent child abuse and violence. The commercial sexual exploitation of children has devastating consequences for these minors, which may include long-lasting physical and psychological trauma, disease (including HIV/AIDS), drug addiction, unwanted pregnancy, malnutrition, social ostracism, and possibly death.

Tourists engaging in CST often travel to developing countries looking for anonymity and the availability of children in prostitution. The crime is typically fueled by weak law enforcement, corruption, the Internet, ease of travel, and poverty. These sexual offenders come from all socio-economic backgrounds and may hold positions of trust. Previous cases of child sex tourism involving U.S. citizens have included a pediatrician, a retired Army sergeant, a dentist and a university professor. Child pornography is frequently involved in these cases; and drugs may also be used to solicit or control the minors.

A Global Response

Over the last five years, there has been an increase in the prosecution of child sex tourism offenses. At least 32 countries have extraterritorial laws that allow the prosecution of their citizens for CST crimes committed abroad. In response to the phenomenon of CST, non-governmental organizations (NGOs), the tourism industry, and governments have begun to address the issue. The World Tourism Organization (WTO) established a task force to combat CST. The WTO, the NGO End Child Prostitution, Child Pornography and Trafficking of Children for Sexual Purposes (ECPAT), and Nordic tour operators created a global Code of Conduct for the Protection of Children from Sexual Exploitation in Travel and Tourism in 1999. As of March 2005, 68 travel companies from 18 countries had signed the code. Many governments have taken commendable steps to combat child sex tourism. For example, France's Ministry of Education and travel industry representatives, developed guidelines on CST for tourism schools and state-owned Air France allocates a portion of in-flight toy sales to fund CST awareness Programmes. Brazil implemented a national awareness campaign on sex tourism. Italy requires tour operators to provide brochures in ticket jackets to travelers regarding its law on child sex offenses both within the country and abroad. Thailand is providing victims with shelter and essential services. The Gambia has created a hotline to which visitors can call to provide information to authorities on sex tourists. Senegal has established a special anti-CST unit within the national police force with offices in two popular tourist destinations. In India's Goa state, film developers must report obscene depictions of children to police. Sweden's Queen Sylvia has made this issue a personal priority and is an effective global advocate.

What the United States Is Doing

In 2003, the United States strengthened its ability to fight child sex tourism by passing the Prosecutorial Remedies and other Tools to end the Exploitation of Children Today (PROTECT) Act and the Trafficking Victim's Protection Reauthorization Act. These laws increase penalties to a maximum of 30 years in prison for engaging in CST. Since the passage of the PROTECT Act, there have been over 20 indictments and over a dozen convictions of child sex tourists. The Department of Homeland

Security has also developed the "Operation Predator" initiative to combat child exploitation, child pornography, and child sex tourism. The United States is also funding the NGO World Vision to conduct major public awareness campaigns overseas that include public service announcements, internet messaging, brochures, posters, and billboards. To bolster interagency, NGO and private sector cooperation, the State Department has designated a point of contact to focus specifically on fighting CST.

To provide information on child sex tourism call the U.S. Immigration and Customs Enforcement tipline at: 1-866-DHS-2ICE.

What Governments Can Do

Enhance Research and Coordination:

- Research the extent and nature of the problem
- Draft an action plan for addressing CST
- Designate a government point of contact to coordinate efforts with non-governmental, intergovernmental, and travel/tourism organizations

Augment Prevention and Training:

- Encourage the travel industry to sign and implement the Code of Conduct
- Fund and/or launch public awareness campaigns, highlighting relevant extraterritorial laws
- Train and sensitize law enforcement on the issue
- Ensure that border and airport officials report any suspected cases of child trafficking

Strengthen Legal Measures and Prosecutions:

- Draft, pass and/or enforce extraterritorial laws criminalizing CST

- Increase punishment for offenders
- Prosecute the crime to the fullest extent possible

Assist Victims:

- Provide shelter, counseling, medical, and legal assistance to victims
- Provide reintegration assistance as appropriate
- Support the efforts of NGOs working with child victims

What United States Citizens Can Do

- Stay informed and support the efforts of authorities and the tourism industry to prevent commercial sexual exploitation of children.
- Report to the authorities abroad and/or to the U.S. Department of Homeland Security's Immigration and Customs Enforcement if you suspect children are being commercially sexually exploited in tourism destinations.
- Be aware that any U.S. citizen or permanent legal resident arrested in a foreign country for sexually abusing minors may be subject to return to the U.S., and if convicted, can face up to 30 years imprisonment.
- Support the efforts of NGOs working to protect children from commercial sexual exploitation.

What Businesses Can Do

Travel, tourism, and hospitality companies can sign the Code of Conduct to Protect Children from Sexual Exploitation in Travel and Tourism, which requires them to implement the following measures:

- Establish a corporate ethical policy against commercial sexual exploitation of children.
- Train tourism personnel.

- Introduce clauses in contracts with suppliers stating a common repudiation of sexual exploitation of children.
- Provide information to travelers through catalogues, brochures, in-flight videos, ticket slips and websites.
- Provide information to local "key persons" at travel destinations.

TOURISM AND CHILD ABUSE: THE CHALLENGES TO MEDIA AND INDUSTRY

Introduction

The conference is a joint initiative of the IFJ and Press Wise to bring together journalists, media professionals, educators, tourism industry representatives and representatives of the workforce to discuss the role of media in combating child sex tourism and to prepare training materials that will assist journalists to produce high quality journalism when reporting violence affecting children.

The IFJ project Reporting Dilemmas: Journalism, Child Rights and Sex Tourism aims to highlight the need for ethical and professional performance in reporting the commercial sexual exploitation of children through sex tourism.

One of the objectives of the project is to develop a common approach between journalists' groups and trade unions covering the workforce in the travel industry on joint information strategies to combat sex tourism.

At the same time a discussion is taking place within the journalistic community of how to respond to the challenge of reporting measures to combat child sex tourism in a professional, informed and comprehensive manner.

The Press Wise pilot project Children, Media, Violence in an Expanding Europe is designed to develop and test guidelines, training materials and training techniques for media professionals to improve the quality and sensitivity of media representations of violence, especially violence affecting children.

The project aims to develop relevant training materials for use in the Czech Republic, France, Spain and the UK, with a view to their implementation within vocational and in-service training across the expanded European Community. Taking as a starting point the IFJ Draft Guidelines on coverage of children's rights, the project has:

- Developed guidance for trainers in the preparation of materials;
- Commissioned annotated bibliographies of research into violence, media and children;
- Held a two-day seminar examining the effects of trauma—physical and sexual abuse, violent crime, war, natural disasters—on children, and the problems faced by journalists in covering such stories.
- Held a two-day seminar on the development of training modules for journalists.

Before the end of 2000 the project will have tested and refined these materials among journalists in the four countries, with a view to encouraging the introduction of sensitisation to such issues within vocational training schemes.

Both issues—child sex tourism and violence and children—pose ethical challenges and dilemmas to journalists. A joint approach to develop guidelines, training materials and joint actions with the tourism industry will result in improved coverage of these issues and can make a difference to the fight against child sex tourism and violence against children.

Background

Growing concern about rights of children at national and international governmental level has in recent years tested the resolve of governments to implement international agreements designed to end the exploitation of children. The UN Convention on the Rights of the Child is already the most widely recognised of any international agreement. Concern over child labour, child prostitution and the civil rights of children are a benchmark by which any nation's commitment to human rights and democracy can be judged.

Raising awareness about the rights of children and the promotion of children's rights is a challenge to media and those who work in journalism. Media must not just report fairly, honestly and accurately on the experience of childhood, but they must also provide space for the diverse, colourful and creative opinions of children themselves.

But respect for childrens' rights is not guaranteed by goodwill alone. The pressures of commercial development, cultural diversity and a global economy that gives easy access for a rich minority to regions where people are struggling to emerge from appalling conditions of poverty and colonial exploitation all continue to define the process by which child rights are implemented.

Child sex tourism is one area particularly recognised as requiring greater action at international and regional level. The role of media is crucial in promoting travel and the richness of the tourism industry. Tourism is the world's leading economic sector and this means that all countries compete to lure visitors. The problem is that in many regions, particularly South Asia and South East Asia, sexual exploitation and particularly the exploitation of children is an unpleasant by-product of the explosion in tourism.

It is an issue that involves many players—journalists and media, travel agents and tourism companies, airlines and travel services, hotel and restaurants and entertainment providers. Until now, there has been little co-operation between these different players in seeking to raise awareness on the issue and in taking practical steps to combat the form of exploitation.

In preparing this project, the IFJ aims to promote new forms of partnership to combat child sex tourism. In particular by:

1. Developing guidelines for journalists in Europe and the regions which highlight the need for ethical and

professional performance in reporting the commercial sexual exploitation of children through sex tourism;

2. Supporting a common approach between journalists' groups and representative trade unions covering the workforce in the travel industry on joint information strategies to combat sex tourism;

3. Initiating a professional dialogue between media specialists in travel and tourism and social affairs journalists on the need for a common approach to professional values in addressing the issue of sex tourism;

4. Organising a European-wide discussion between the tourism industry, media specialists in travel and representatives of the industry workforce on actions required to enhance media performance in coverage of actions in defence of children subject to sexual exploitation.

In the preparation for this conference concerns organizations have been involved in two important discussions.

The first, in January 2000, brought together industry workforce representatives, media specialists and journalists' groups to consider strategies for extending journalistic sources of information and developing a common approach to actions to combat child sex tourism.

The second, held in August 2000, involved experts from two key areas of journalistic expertise: travel and tourism specialists and correspondents covering social affairs, including rights of the child, with journalism educators. The exchange focused on ways of improving inter-media liaison on coverage of sex tourism issues in Europe and looked at priorities for raising awareness within journalism training structures in Europe.

These meetings agreed that action is needed in a number of key areas to raise awareness of child sex tourism issues, to promote inter-industry liaison on ways of combating child sex tourism, and reinforcing guidelines for journalists on sex tourism questions. Some draft recommendations are contained within this report.

One aim of our meeting is to prepare a text for European journalism associations and unions, media organisations and journalism training establishments that will identify standards required for sensitivity and ethical reporting related to sex tourism and the commercial sexual exploitation of children.

It is hoped that this text will be published and disseminated to media and journalists' associations and unions in the major European union languages

The crucial issue is to raise awareness. Journalists themselves are too often ignorant of child rights issues and unaware of how media contribute, often unknowingly, to the commercial process that encourages sexual exploitation of children.

The preparatory meetings found that existing efforts to combat child sex tourism are virtually unknown inside journalism. The existence of the World Tourism Organisation Globe Code of Ethics for Tourism, for instance, which was adopted in Chile last year, remains largely unknown inside journalism, even within the high-profile circles of travel journalism. The WTO code states:

> *Article 2 (2)*—"Tourism activities should respect the equality of men and women; they should promote human rights and, more particularly, the individual rights of the most vulnerable groups, notably children…"

> *Article 2 (3)*—The exploitation of human beings in any form, particularly sexual, especially when applied to children, conflicts with the fundamental aims of tourism and is the negation of tourism, as such, in accordance with international law, it should be energetically combated…and penalised without concession by the national legislation of both the countries visited and countries of the perpetrators of these acts, even when they are carried out abroad."

This Code and its contents was the subject of detailed review and discussion in Israel a few days ago organized by the World Tourism Organisation, focusing on implementation of the aims of the code.

At the same time the IFJ and its member organisations have spent some time in framing guidelines for journalists that set out practical lines of professional action and consideration in the area of child rights. These guidelines were adopted at a conference in Brazil two years (see below).

One issue to be considered at the meeting will be how effective are codes and guidelines and what actions need to be taken to enforce the worthy ideals and aspirations of such texts.

Strong commercial motives, primarily the need to win audiences and advertisers, influence the content of mass media communication and this is particularly true in the area of tourism, one of the world's richest industrial sectors. Advertising is also subject to a combination of legislation and self-regulation in the way it appeals to children.

It is impossible to properly consider action without examining the commercial pressures on the industry at all levels. There is a need for investment in strategies that will expose commercial sexual exploitation and, by doing so, reinforce public confidence in tourism.

At the same time efforts continue to set standards in the existing world of media technology, the development of new forms of communication such as the Internet open up opportunities for paedophiles and pornographers that raise international concern. The major problem in controlling Internet material is that nobody controls it. However, recent action against pedophile networks show that online services are no safe haven.

The online world provides great opportunities for sexual predators to exploit children. All sides of the discussion related to sexual tourism need to consider how to establish standards and strategies that protect children and empower young people themselves to exercise more control over the on-line world.

The Challenge to Journalism

Whether it is news and current affairs, or the more complex world of the creative and performing arts, all media professionals and the organisations for which they work have a responsibility to recognise that children's rights concern them.

But how do we raise awareness? To answer this question requires serious examination of the way media work, of how existing principles of accountability apply, and how media must be freed from reins of political and economic control which limit professionalism and undermine ethical standards.

Irrespective of external pressure, the media role in the evolution of children's rights is complex. On the one hand, news media tell the stories of abused and abuser, through news reports, photographs, documentaries, and drama. But on the other, they can themselves become the exploiter, for instance by creating sexually provocative images of children in news or advertising, or, at worst, as the vehicle for child pornography, or sources of information for pedophile networks, something of particular concern in the age of Internet.

Furthermore, the way the media portray children has a profound impact on society's attitude to children and childhood, which also affects the way adults behave. Even the images children themselves see, especially of sex and violence, influence their expectation of their role in life.

Media professionals need to consider these questions, even if there are no easy answers to complex issues or to ethical dilemmas. There are standards and benchmarks by which media can judge how they portray children in society. In the conclusion of this section are a number of practical recommendations intended to make media and journalists more responsive and to encourage debate within media about the portrayal of children and their rights.

Looking particularly at child sex tourism, internal editorial arrangements within media sometimes are sometimes an obstacle to good coverage and better understanding of issues.

In most established and mainstream media travel journalism is an important area of editorial activity. But it is organised quite separately from the editorial departments dealing with social policy and rights of children. Journalists in these two areas of work rarely meet.

As a result, while the travel department of any media organisation adds strongly to the advertising and commercial strength of media, very rarely does travel journalism draw attention to the problems of child sex tourism. Too little attention is paid to the predatory nature of commercial sexual exploitation in many exotic destinations.

One challenge is to examine how editorial practice can be improved to bring social and children's issues into the framework of travel reporting.

The important role that media play in raising public awareness of children's rights is well understood, but journalism is an ambiguous partner. While media help to uncover cases of abuse of children and their rights and to raise awareness of the problem they also infiltrate the public with tolerant attitudes towards child pornography and prostitution or provide the means (for example advertisements) by which gratification may be achieved.

Journalists need to be aware of the consequences of their reporting. Sensational coverage often distorts and exploits a serious problem, perhaps doing more harm than good, but often the response of editors will be that they are trying to fulfil the responsibility to cover serious social issues, while continuing to turn a profit. Sensationalism, they argue, permits an important but unpleasant topic to be covered in such a way that it still captures the readers' and viewers' attention.

However, this does not answer the need for more analysis of the social and economic causes of commercial sexual exploitation of children: the corrupt employers, the pimps, the drug culture, the parents in poverty who are proud to have sold their children for a sum which will enable them to support the rest of the family.

Nevertheless, media can broaden the scope of reporting. The positive story of children, their lives and their rights is not being told in full. To examine how this can be changed requires examination of the professional conditions in which media work, a review of the principles or guidelines journalists and programme-makers should follow, and the obstacles--legal, financial, or cultural—that stand in the way of good journalism.

A starting point for good reporting is freedom of information. Journalists are only ever as good as their sources of information. Reporting on child rights and tourism requires access to a great deal of information about children, much of it held by the state authorities. Media cannot report effectively if information about education, health, employment, development and social conditions is not made generally available. In too many countries, governments and state institutions are secretive and hoard information. Citizens have a right to freedom of information. Without it, media cannot report accurately on the reality of children's lives.

Respect, too, for independent journalism is an essential condition for a media culture of openness about children and their rights. For example, journalists recognise that betraying sources not only inhibits their own ability to investigate; it also makes it more difficult for every journalist to work, and may even put their lives at risk, as well as the safety of the informants.

Many of the professional obligations of journalists are set out in codes of professional conduct. But how effective are voluntary codes and guidelines? The simple answer is the same as that for all forms of self-regulation—it depends upon the professional confidence of journalists, their knowledge of the issues they are dealing with, and the conditions in which they work.

A recent world-wide study of codes carried out by Presswise for the IFJ reveals that journalists' organisations until recently had few specific codes of good practice for covering the rights of children. To remedy this in May 1998 the International Federation of Journalists launched the first international guidelines for journalists covering children's rights at a conference attended by journalists from 70 countries. Regional discussion on these guidelines have already taken place in Latin America and Africa and further consultation is planned in Asia with a second world conference to take place in 2001.

The aim of this code—which is attached to this section—is to ensure accuracy and sensitivity among journalists when reporting on issues involving children. The code get to the core of people's concerns when it comes to how media deal with the children, including:

- Sexual, violent or victim-focused programming and images that are potentially damaging to children;
- Stereotypes and sensational presentation of journalistic material;
- Media failure to consider the consequences of publication and to minimise harm to children;
- Respect for the privacy of children and protection of their identity unless it is demonstrably in the public interest;
- The need to give children access to media to express their own opinions;
- The obligation to verify information before publication.

The challenge to journalists and media in addressing these problems is to be aware of their responsibilities and to promote improvements. While codes cannot guarantee ethical reporting, they do identify the professional dilemmas that journalists and media face when reporting on the rights of children.

Fierce commercial competition is one factor leading media to exploit victims. The exposure of emotions and sensationalisation of events attract audiences and sell news. Cash-conscious media organisations apply greater pressure on news teams for productivity. Journalists, therefore, sometimes take the ill-considered, easy route to newsgathering, perpetuating the sorts of myth and stereotype identified above.

But in all this there are many examples of good journalism that act as a counter-weight to media indifference and lack of awareness. There is a need for media to identify good practice, to applaud high standards and to encourage improved coverage. Journalism prizes, organised at national, regional and international level can do much if they are used to stimulate debate and dialogue.

Recommendations For Raising Awareness in Media and Promotion of Action to Combat Child Sex Tourism

Media professionals need to develop strategies that strengthen the role of media in providing information on all aspects of the children's rights, but particularly dealing with child sex tourism.

The following recommendations are designed to raise awareness about the importance of this issue:

1. Training for journalists and Media Education
   (a) Materials outlining the Convention on the Rights of the Child and its implications for media as well as examples of good practice within media can form the basis of training courses and manuals for journalists and other media professionals.
   (b) Training seminars focused on issues related to violence against children and commercial sexual exploitation of children, including through tourism, should be organised to raise awareness within media of these issues.
2. Creating the Conditions for Professional Journalism
   (a) Industry partners, workforce representatives and tourism authorities should work with media and other civil society groups to create the conditions for legitimate journalistic inquiry and monitoring of how children can be adversely affected by tourism arrangements.
   (b) Media professionals should recognise that freedom of expression must go hand in hand with other fundamental human rights, including freedom from exploitation and intimidation. They should

give careful consideration to the facts when weighing up the relative merits of the different claims, and not allow themselves to be swayed by commercial or political considerations;

(c) Dialogue between media organisations, journalists, the tourism worforce and industry representatives should be supported to highlight problems and concerns and better understanding of the needs of journalists and media when reporting children's issues related to tourism.

(d) Structures for Dialogue involving industry, the workforce and media should include a process of regular review of Codes of Ethics and Journalistic Guidelines to ensure that they are effective and enforced.

(e) National NGOs, workforce organisations and industry representatives should consider compiling a directory of reliable experts on the rights of children and related topics, to be distributed to media. Such information could also be accessible on computer data banks.

3. Codes of Conduct and Self Regulation

(a) Codes of conduct and reporting guidelines can be useful in demonstrating that something needs to be done. Specific guidelines on child rights reporting, such as those adopted by the IFJ, should be drawn up by professional associations to accompany their general ethical codes and should draw attention to issues regarding violence against children and commercial sexual exploitation.

(b) Journalists and programme-makers have a duty to increase public awareness of the violation of children's rights. However, reporting needs to be carried out with enormous care. In particular, media should adhere to the highest standards of professional conduct when reporting on the rights of children.

(c) They should avoid, or challenge, the myths and stereotypes that surround children, particularly those from developing countries. For instance, the myth that parents in developing countries do not value their children; that girls are inferior to boys; that children are drawn into crime through their own fault; or that child labour and sex tourism alleviate poverty for the victim, or the host nation.

(d) Journalists should never publish details that put vulnerable children at risk. Journalists should take particular care not to reveal information that damages the dignity of children, and avoid identifying them, while at the same time telling their stories in a compelling and newsworthy way.

4. The Need for Newsroom Debate

(a) A constructive and supportive debate should be encouraged between media professionals, about reporting of travel and tourism and children's rights and media images of children. Such dialogue should take place between media managements, editorial departments and marketing sections.

(b) Media organisations should consider regular review of travel coverage and set it in the context of coverage of social policy as it affects children both at home and abroad. This issue should be put to specialist 'children's correspondents', or journalists with responsibility for covering all aspects of children's lives.

Brussels, September 29th-October 1st 2000

This meeting is a joint activity of two projects currently supported by the European Commission. These are Children, Media, Violence in an Expanding Europe and Reporting Dilemmas: Journalists and Child Sex Tourism, both of which are supported by The International Federation of Journalists and The PressWise Trust.

Chapter 5

Model Tourism Action Plans: Commenwealth, Anglesey, Wellington and Canada

COMMENWEALTH TOURISM ACTION

Commonwealth tourism ministers, who met for the first time in Kuala Lumpur, Malaysia, last week (19 to 21 March 2004) have developed an action plan to promote tourism and information exchange. The plan includes the establishment of a Commonwealth Centre for Tourism Promotion (CCTP) and the organisation of workshops to identify joint marketing and promotional activities between the public and private sector. A task force formed at the meeting will study the role of the CCTP and work out its functions as well as identify the sources of financing to run it.

"The task force will consist of representatives from all regions of the Commonwealth and be chaired by the Commonwealth Secretariat," said Malaysia's Minister for Culture, Arts and Tourism Dato' Paduka Abdul Kadir Sheik Fadzir, who chaired the meeting.

"The members will have until the end of the year to recommend to governments the terms of reference and the work plan of the proposed centre. It will create an information database and co-ordinate an information exchange, which will contribute towards a collaborative approach to tourism marketing and promotion."

The tourism ministers also agreed to work closely with the World Tourism Organisation and the World Travel and Tourism Council on trade liberalisation issues. They underscored the importance of tourism in reducing poverty and promoting investment, exports and jobs. Socio-cultural understanding and peace are also enhanced by tourism.

The ministers supported the international community's fight against terrorism and other criminal activities affecting the tourism sector. They noted the impact of these actions on trans-border movement of people, transport and economic flows. They also recognised the problems faced by some member countries in complying with international standards of safety and security, and called on donor agencies to assist.

The importance of sustainable tourism was highlighted, particularly for small and vulnerable states, and the ministers stressed the need for concrete actions to strengthen this sector. They agreed to incorporate tourism as a priority in development and poverty reduction strategies.

Secretary-General Don McKinnon and tourism can play a key role in transforming the lives of the poor as it is one of the key instruments of economic development. Speaking at the opening ceremony in Kuala Lumpur last week, he said, "For many nations in the Commonwealth, including small states and developing countries, tourism is not only an important source of income, it plays an essential part in their efforts to lift themselves out of poverty. A vibrant tourism industry brings inward investment, foreign exchange earnings and stimulates employment. It is often a boon for small and medium enterprises. For them, tourism is one of the key access routes into the global economy."

ACTION PLAN FOR TOURISM IN ANGLESEY

Introduction

Anglesey is a rural island with a population of 66,000. It's tourism industry attracts 2 million visitors to the island per annum, accounting for £181 million into the local economy and supports 19 per cent of employment. It is considered to be an important sector in the island's economic base and is recognised as one sector which is capable of sustainable growth and thus a vital element of future economic well being.

However the present industry is based on a relatively short season of traditional family holidays providing low income and limited reinvestment. This situation is compounded by a fragmented sector of small and micro businesses competing for an ever declining volume of visitors as the global tourism market and variety of holiday opportunities expands.

Anglesey has a very diverse nature, a characteristic that can be harnessed to provide new and additional tourism opportunities and benefit from developing tourism trends for short break and special interest holidays. It is geologically an ancient island, with a variety of recognised natural assets, its coastline is all designated an Area of Outstanding Natural Beauty or Heritage Coast which provides the basis for beach and coastal holidays. It has, at present, 22 award winning beaches. It is rich in heritage and culture with a wealth of prehistoric, Roman, mediaeval, and industrial artefacts, and traditionally has a range of manmade tourist attractions mainly geared to the family holiday sector.

Recent tourism projects, mainly developed through the Leader II initiative, aimed at developing niche markets within the special interest sectors such as walking, cycling, golf fishing and farm holidays, have illustrated that modest investment in such areas can provide significant benefits. The challenge is to ensure that such projects do not develop in isolation but in such a way as to be sustainable and provide benefits to the widest possible range of local businesses and communities.

Whereas the tourism sector demonstrates many of the characteristics of other SMEs, the industry possesses unique characteristics which cannot always be addressed comfortably within mainstream business support. It also impacts considerably on the environment and local communities and has considerable implications for infrastructure. The Action

Plan for Tourism will therefore identify the needs and aspirations of the tourism trade on the island and balance them with the requirements of the visitor to maximise benefits to the SMEs and increase employment opportunities.

This will be done by maximising the synergy with the broader regional and local programmes and providing sector specific assistance where these programmes are not appropriate for the special needs of this business sector.

Strategic Objective

To develop a range of tourism strategies and programmes which ensure the sustained development of tourism on the Island and maximise the benefits it provides to the local economy.

This will be achieved through:

- Exploiting training and business development mechanisms to create high-quality employment opportunities and enable existing tourism SMEs to develop.
- Improving the overall standard and variety of the tourism product/service that is provided.
- Enabling the industry to prosper from the island's natural diversity.
- Developing marketing and promotional activities together with information provision in a manner whichmeets the needs and expectations of the customer.

Links to Other Strategies and Documentation

The economic importance of tourism has been recognised by the National Assembly for Wales within the recently approved National Tourism Strategy—"Achieving our Potential". The strategy was produced by the Wales Tourist Board (WTB) following extensive consultation with the public sector and establishments that are operating within the industry and The main objectives of the strategy are to:

- To market Wales more effectively as an attractive all year round tourism destination.

- To exceed the expectations of visitors to Wales by providing high standards and ensuring that investment in tourism is responsive to changing needs.

- To improve professionalism and innovation by raising the profile of the industry and by enhancing skills, training and motivation within the industry.

- To embrace a sustainable approach to tourism development which benefits society, involves local communities and enhances Wales' unique environmental and cultural assets.

- The Regional Tourism Strategy—"Co-operating to Compete", co-funded by the WTB and covering the six unitary authority areas of North Wales is a key component within the national strategy.

It's overall strategic aim is to:

Contribute to winning a bigger market share for Wales as a whole from both domestic and overseas markets. This will be achieved by extending the North Wales vision 'Co-operating to Compete' so that both product development and marketing campaigns are carefully planned and targeted to work in a complementary way.

On a local level, the Isle of Anglesey Economic Development Strategy, Unitary Development Plan (Draft version), which reocgnise the local importance of toursim have been paramount to the plans development.

In addition, results fromby the 'Ynys Môn Visitors Survey' (1997-1998) have provided valuable information and customer profiles/expectations in relation to the tourism product on Anglesey. It has illustrated that the tourism industry on Anglesey, while providing for traditional holidays, is not adapting to the changing tourism market and is thus losing market share. The undertaking of the 'Scarborough Tourism

Economic Activity Model' which was begun last year is also providing information on the economic value of tourism and an insight into changing trends.

Analysis of the available information, together with the strategic framework provided by wider policies and programmes has provided the strong foundation upon which this Plan has been based.

Links with Other Local Action Plans

Many of the issues which underpin the tourism industry are also commonplace in other sectors and industries. The support, development, training and skills issues are uniform. As a result, it is envisaged that businesses operating within the tourism industry will benefit directly from the programmes outlined within the Business Action Plan. Additionally, ruraland community development issues are also relevant to the future growth of tourism on Anglesey.

These clear and important links represent the need to synergise and co-ordinate activities and programmes which are outlined in other strands of the Local Action Plan with the needs of the tourism industry. This approach will also reduce duplication of both effort and resources.

Links with the Single Programme Document (SPD)

This Plan relates closely to the Aims and Objectives which are outlined within the SPD. The wide ranging nature and requirements of the industry make it likely that the programmes outlined within this plan will seek funding assistance from a number of Measures within Priorities 1, 2, 4, 5 and 6.

Tourism Action Plan Projects

Developing Local Knowledge

Aims and Objectives

- To develop a wider knowledge of Anglesey and its attractions by local businesses and residents.

- To provide a knowledge base that can be passed on to visitors and potential tourists to:
  - ◻ To increase the numbers of visitors to the island and encourage them to stay on the island.
  - ◻ To increase tourism activity across the island.
  - ◻ To increase the spread of economic and (social) benefits to local businesses and communities.
  - ◻ To create ambassadors for the island within both business and tourism.
- To develop better networking and the opportunity for mutual support and joint business initiatives.
- To undertake a pilot research project that can be used to test and evaluate a range of methodologies with a view to developing a more comprehensive range of activities to support future development and promotion of tourism on the Isle of Anglesey.
- To encourage residents and local people to take more leisure visits in their own locality.
- To establish a database for the development and implementation of the Tourism Action Plan.

Project Description

The project will undertake three related pilot schemes that will target different sectors of business and the community to raise the level of local awareness and knowledge of tourist related businesses.

Each scheme will allow access to tourism related businesses to:

- Gain first hand knowledge of the business *e.g.* enabling local people to pass on information to visitors
- Provide the opportunity for developing networking and mutual support activities *e.g.* pass on business to local providers etc.
- Provide the opportunities for developing joint business activities and marketing.

Scheme 1: Island wide and provide the opportunity for residents and the staff of businesses to experience tourist attractions.

Scheme 2: Sector based, providing business to business support and experience to encourage networking and best practice.

Scheme 3: Community based providing different businesses and specific local people based in the locality to learn more about each other and encourage mutual support and networking opportunities.

The schemes will test different methodologies including voucher schemes over a fixed period of time, informal targeted invitations, and formal tours and presentations. It will include the employment of a dedicated project officer and administration staff to ensure the support and encouragement that small and micro businesses will need to enable them to participate.

The main purpose is to be as inclusive as possible and raise the awareness of tourism to a wide audience. This will then provide a receptive base for the development of other tourism projects to raise the quality of the tourism product on Anglesey and develop a sustainable tourism industry spreading benefits to a wide range of businesses and communities.

Outputs

If implemented it is envisaged that the project in total will involve and assist up to 200 businesses. and enable 2000 visits to be to be made. Scheme 3 include the involvement of 5 communities across the island.

Funding

Funding will be secured via the businesses themselves in the form of agreed levels of goods and services and via the local authority in the form of financial assistance and office time.

Green and Clean

Aims and Objectives

- To provide a range of opportunities. to upgrade the general image of the island to the visitor.
- To raise the awareness of local businesses, communities and individuals of the need to clean up and enhance their locality.
- Encourage, facilitate and market clean up campaigns, develop environmental awareness, encourage recycling.
- Develop the use of rural skills such as stone walling and hedge laying and reintroduce the concept of lengths men to provide opportunities for local employment.
- Develop local footpaths and bridle ways.
- Link activities to job creation and skills development programmes.
- Link administration and funding to local communities to encourage community development and ownership.
- Provide for project managers and co-ordinators.

Project Description

To develop a range of co-ordinated activities that will link with training and community development schemes to increase the quality of life within communities and develop local initiatives and pride.

Provide a range of job opportunities and economic benefits to rural areas. Increase the quality of tourism and support other activities to increase visitor numbers to the island.

An Island for All Seasons

Aims and Objectives

- To provide a range of tourism trails, based on sectoral, thematic and geographic areas to encourage visitors to travel around the area or the island.

- To encourage use of different means of travel including cycling, walking, horseback and boats.
- To support the development of new and existing attractions and facilities to provide for a range of attractive, themed trails.
- To provide the mechanisms for an integrated tourist information network across the island utilizing new and existing print, information technology, TICs and the development of new tourist information points within local businesses and communities.
- To provide opportunities for businesses to gain knowledge and training in relation to tourism and local product knowledge.

Project Description

To develop, support and market a range of niche tourism products which will build on the existing diversity of the Isle of Anglesey as a tourism product to provide economic benefits and employment opportunities to businesses and geographic areas of the island. To undertake a series of co-ordinated activities to support these developments and develop the tourist potential of the island. Facilitate the development of co-ordinated information utilising local businesses to supplement national and strategic activities including the development of a local pocket guide, the development of auto and audio tours and multilingual print and information. Work within developing national and regional training programmes to provide a scheme of opportunities to develop and support businesses on Anglesey. Provide additional training to add value through knowledge of a local perspective.

DEVELOPING TOURISM ACTION PLAN: A CASE STUDY OF WELLINGTON 421

The Vision

Positively Wellington Tourism seeks to position Wellington as a destination of choice domestically and internationally and be regarded as the most vibrant, innovative and creative centre for tourism marketing and development in New Zealand.

It will achieve this by paying attention to both product development and marketing.

Product development is a strategic priority for Wellington's tourism industry. The city has a number of key attractions, but more 365-day per year commissionable product is central to achieving Positively Wellington Tourism's vision. Critical to this will be developments such as the Karori Wildlife Sanctuary and the Marine Conservation Centre.

The development of key infrastructure such as the proposed Multi-Sport Stadium and a purpose-built Convention Centre as well as the Waterfront will also be important. Better infrastructure will help develop a comprehensive events calendar for Wellington. A solid offering of events is crucial in the context of a maturing visitor destination such as Wellington. Over time, however, this may become less important as year-round attractions and activities develop.

Positively Wellington Tourism must continually refine and develop the way it markets the city. It seeks to develop cutting edge marketing programmes which are effective both domestically and internationally and target both the leisure and the business traveller. The internet, conferences, conventions and events will continue to be key tools in Positively Wellington Tourism's marketing programme.

Cultural tourism is recognised as a key driver of the Interactive Traveller. Positively Wellington Tourism will continue to work with Central Government and the wider industry to strengthen and market Wellington's cultural tourism offering. This will lead to exciting product developments and increased depth of product in the cultural tourism sector.

The marketing initiative 'nature close to the city' will help drive international visitation and is an attractive proposition for Tourism New Zealand's Interactive Traveller target. This initiative leverages Wellington's stunning natural areas, such as the South Coast, in contrast to the vibrancy, creativity and energy of the city.

A shared understanding with Wellington City Council is essential to achieving the vision. Council's Creative City, Innovation Capital initiative is well aligned with Wellington's market position as the arts and culture capital of New Zealand.

Marketing Vision 2004–2009

Positively Wellington Tourism aims to see:

- Wellington as one of the top three destinations visited in New Zealand by international visitors.
- Wellington regarded by international travel trade as a 'must-see' destination.
- Wellington rated by at least 80 per cent of domestic market as the 'hottest' city to visit in New Zealand.
- Highly active marketing programme operating in Australia, with 200,000 visitors from Australia and Wellington regarded by Australians as a must-see destination.
- Visitor Information Centre fully integrated into overall marketing function and delivery of Positively Wellington Tourism's marketing and product development programmes.
- Wellington as New Zealand's leading events destination with a calendar of events that addresses low and shoulder season travel.
- Wellington as a leading conference destination with astrong market presence in New Zealand and Australia.
- Wellington leading e-commerce trading in the tourism industry with the most active RTO website in New Zealand.

Positively Wellington Tourism Aims to See the 2004 Core Develop and Expend

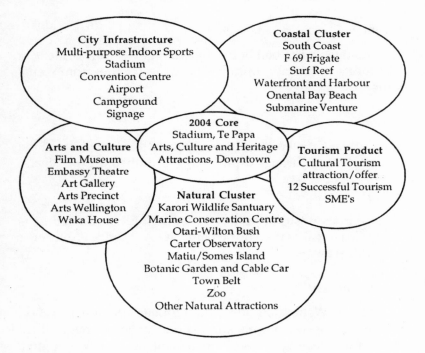

City Infrastructure
Multi-purpose Indoor Sports Stadium
Convention Centre
Airport
Campground
Signage

Coastal Cluster
South Coast
F 69 Frigate
Surf Reef
Waterfront and Harbour
Onental Bay Beach
Submarine Venture

2004 Core
Stadium, Te Papa
Arts, Culture and Heritage
Attractions, Downtown

Arts and Culture
Film Museum
Embassy Theatre
Art Gallery
Arts Precinct
Arts Wellington
Waka House

Tourism Product
Cultural Tourism
attraction/offer
12 Successful Tourism
SME's

Natural Cluster
Karori Wildlife Santuary
Marine Conservation Centre
Otari-Wilton Bush
Carter Observatory
Matiu/Somes Island
Botanic Garden and Cable Car
Town Belt
Zoo
Other Natural Attractions

Setting the Scene

Positively Wellington Tourism: Leading the Way

Positively Wellington Tourism aims to be an inspirational and innovative leader in the tourism industry and to continue to help tourism add even greater value to the Wellington economy and community.

Positively Wellington Tourism is essentially a marketing body whose purpose it is to maximise the contribution tourism can make to Wellington City's economy and lifestyle. Positively Wellington Tourism also takes a lead role advocating and supporting product and infrastructural development in a bid to add further depth to the industry.

Brand Wellington

Wellington's key brand elements are:

Creativity

Wellington is a hot-bed of creative thought. This is evident in all aspects of the city, from public art to theatre, from scenic tours to shopping.

Nationhood

The Capital City, Wellington is uniquely positioned to tell the nation's history through captivating and authentic experiences.

Accessible Nature

Wellington's position between a stunning harbour and the South Coast makes it a natural paradise—yet coffee is only ever a short trip away.

City Excitement

Downtown Wellington offers the ultimate urban experience. Shopping, cafes, bars, restaurants and entertainment all fill Downtown creating a sense of excitement unique to Wellington.

Strategic Context

To achieve its objectives, Positively Wellington Tourism must work collaboratively with Wellington City Council and other public agencies to promote Wellington as a destination. As a core funder of Positively Wellington Tourism and a key developer of infrastructure vital to the sector, Wellington City Council is a vital partner.

Positively Wellington Tourism will also continue to work in partnership with strategic allies such as hotels, airlines, tourism operators and Wellington City retailers. Other mportant partners include Tourism New Zealand, New Zealand Tourism

Industry Association, the National Tourism Strategy working group, Regional Wellington, Centre Stage of New Zealand and Positively Wellington Business.

Positively Wellington Tourism can not achieve success without the support of the city and the wider industry.

Shared Strategies

The Tourism Action Plan takes account of current national and regional strategic plans, while addressing issues specific to Wellington.

Nothing will happen in isolation. The following are examples of strategic alignment Positively Wellington Tourism will seek at city, regional and national levels.

At a city level, Wellington City Council's Creative City Innovation Capital initiative, launched in 2003, fits with the positioning of Wellington as the arts, heritage and culture Capital.

- Positively Wellington Tourism will work to leverage the Creative City Innovation Capital initiative in its own visitor marketing programmes.
- Tourism partners will be encouraged to incorporate the initiative into their strategic thinking.

At a regional level, Positively Wellington Tourism will continue to promote the wider Wellington region as part of its involvement with Centre Stage of New Zealand, the international marketing collective comprising Wairarapa, Nelson, Marlborough and the Wellington region.

- Positively Wellington Tourism, in line with Tourism New Zealand's strategy, will target the Interactive Traveller in its international marketing.
- Offshore activity will continue to be delivered under the Centre Stage regional model, with its focus on Wellington's primary markets of Australia, USA and UK.

- Positively Wellington Tourism will continue to market to the visiting friends and relatives market.
- Product development will continue to be a key focus of Positively Wellington Tourism.

At a national level, Tourism New Zealand's cultural tourism strategy is complementary with Wellington's emphasis on arts and culture.

- Positively Wellington Tourism will work to maximise and improve the cultural tourism offering in Wellington.

Tourism Growth

In the last ten years, Wellington has developed into one of New Zealand's top three visitor destinations. Visitor nights now exceed 3.5 million per year.

The construction of New Zealand's national museum, Te Papa Tongarewa in 1998, provided a flagship tourism attraction. Te Papa now attracts 1.3 million visitors annually and is the biggest visitor attraction in New Zealand. Te Papa has contributed significantly to Wellington's tourism industry and will continue to be a key driver of both international and domestic visitation.

Infrastructural developments, such as the world-class Westpac Stadium and upgraded Wellington International Airport, have also helped lift the tourism industry to new levels of success.

On the back of these developments, Wellington's accommodation sector has grown and visitor nights in commercial accommodation have risen. New hotels, serviced apartments and backpacker accommodation are testament to this.

Positively Wellington Tourism's marketing, both to the international and domestic markets, have contributed to the industry's growth.

Increased confidence in Wellington's ability to perform as a tourism destination has led to greater private sector investment. A number of smaller tourism businesses have begun operating in the past two years and there has been particular growth in tour businesses. However, more private sector investment is critical to increasing the tourism product offering and so improving the visitor experience in Wellington.

International events hosted in Wellington have highlighted the city's ability to host large numbers of visitors and have helped put Wellington on the international map. Such events include the International Rugby Sevens, Global Challenge Yacht Race—which will stop over at Wellington for the third time in 2005, the Asian Patent Attorney's Association Conference and the World Premiere of *The Lord of the Rings: The Return of the King*.

Although great progress has been made, Wellington is still a maturing destination. Huge scope remains to build on the successes of the city's growing tourism industry.

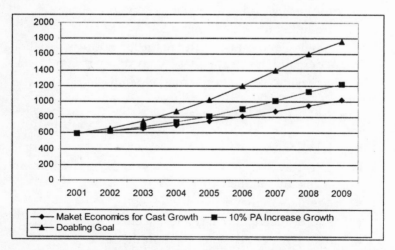

Note: This graph represents three different forecast growth targets.

The Market Economics Ltd figure represents the national forecasts for growth in the city.

The 10 per cent per annum Increase Growth line is what Positively Wellington Tourism believes is achievable by 2006 and beyond.

The Doubling Goal is Positively Wellington Tourism's 'stretch target'. It represents a doubling of the Market Economics Ltd. forecast growth figure.

Key Aims and Objectives

The overall aim of the Tourism Action Plan is:

To maximise the contribution that the tourism sector makes to Wellington's economy and community by positioning Wellington as a competitive and appealing destination in the domestic and global tourism market.

It is guided by five strategic pillars of success:

- Identifying and assisting in the development of new product.
- Supporting and championing new infrastructure.
- Strengthening Downtown retail vitality.
- Growing domestic tourism to further address variations in demand, including seasonality and weekend issues.
- Increasing international market share.

The goals of the pillars are to:

- Help enhance the visitor experience.
- Help develop a strong, professional, profitable and sustainable industry.
- Stimulate demand for businesses.
- Be productive in marketing the city.
- Ensure better alignment within the sector.

These pillars will help ensure the strategy is delivered. Positively Wellington Tourism will continue to pursue these pillars with a high degree of focus.

Identifying and Assisting in the Development of New Product

Positively Wellington Tourism will continue to facilitate and support the development of a range of new and existing visitor attractions and commissionable products. It will, in particular, support the development of those products that align with Wellington's core brand strengths of creativity, nationhood, accessible nature and city excitement. It will also support those that have a link with the Creative City Innovative Capital vision.

Positively Wellington Tourism will continue to take a destination management approach to developing Wellington's tourism industry. Part of this will involve taking into account short, medium and long term industry needs, whilst focusing on the development of a socially, economically and environmentally sustainable sector.

This approach is being worked into Positively Wellington Tourism's business plan and is reflected throughout its marketing initiatives.

Positively Wellington Tourism sees the following as adding significant value to the industry:

- The Karori Wildlife Sanctuary
- Nature based tourism product
- South Coast marketing and development
- Marine Conservation Centre
- Cultural tourism attraction and development

Supporting and Championing New Infrastructure

Sound infrastructure is the basis upon which Wellington can achieve ultimate tourism success.

Positively Wellington Tourism views the following infrastructure as important to overall industry growth:

- Better visitor signage and interpretation
- Multi-purpose Indoor Sports Stadium
- Waterfront Development

- Purpose-built Convention Centre
- Increased capacity and frequency of air access
- CBD Campervan facility

Strengthening Downtown Retail Competitiveness

Downtown Wellington is the premier shopping, dining and entertainment destination in New Zealand. It is one of Wellington's top tourism products.

Positively Wellington Tourism will help maximise the contribution Downtown Wellington makes to the tourism industry by:

- Continuing to evolve and grow Downtown and Four Quarter branding.
- Continuing to position Downtown as central to Wellington's visitor experience.
- Continuing to contribute to Wellington City Council's vision to ensure Downtown Wellington delivers "Absolutely the best Downtown experience".
- Continuing to support events that celebrate and enhance the Downtown Wellington experience and brand, such as the Wellington Fashion Festival.
- Growing Downtown's share of Wellington's retail sales.

Growing Domestic Tourism to Further Address Seasonality and Weekend Issues and Extending the Brand

Positively Wellington Tourism will continue to aggressively target the domestic market with strategic campaigns using a three pronged approach. This will focus on the weekend leisure traveller, the VFR market and events including conferences.

Key actions Positively Wellington Tourism must take to maintain and grow competitiveness in the domestic market include:

- Continue to develop the Positively Wellington and Visiting Friends and Relatives campaigns.

- Maintain a strong presence in the domestic conference market, using conferences and conventions to generate low and shoulder season trade.

- Continue to develop products and offers for the 1-5 hour drive market.

- Maintain a strong marketing presence in the domestic education market.

- Extend Wellington's brand presence and strengthen the Arts and Culture market.

- Continue to develop a strong year-round calendar of events that will attract visitors.

- Maintain a strong marketing presence on the internet and use the website to push on-line sales.

Increasing International Market Share

Wellington is an appealing destination for Tourism New Zealand's Interactive Traveller target. It offers a sophisticated and cultural city experience within close proximity of stunning natural attractions.

Key actions Positively Wellington Tourism must take to maintain and grow competitiveness in the international market are:

- Continue to grow the "Centre Stage of New Zealand regional marketing alliance and other partnerships.

- Actively build Wellington's profile amongst consumers and trade in the Australian market.

- Pro-actively build Wellington's brand positioning as the capital city that is vibrant, cosmopolitan, situated centrally in New Zealand and within easy access to nature.

- Build onshore activity to target international visitors. This includes increasing Wellington's presence in visitor centres, backpackers and locations where travellers on less structured itineraries can more clearly identify what Wellington has to offer.

- Help ensure the experience and offer Interactive Travellers receive in Wellington is second to none and builds on "surprise and delight" factor to gain increased length of stay and positive word of mouth.
- Maintain a strong marketing presence on the internet and use the website to push on-line sales.
- Target mid-sized conferences (100 to 500 delegates) especially from Australia.
- Target the international visiting friends and relatives (VFR) market, especially out of Australia and the UK, in partnership with tourism and non-tourism partners.

The Markets

While the international and the domestic visitor markets are both important to Wellington, each carries its own needs. Positively Wellington Tourism must take into account the expectations and travel motivations of both markets to meet their different needs and so achieve ultimate tourism success.

Positively Wellington Tourism is aware of increasing competition from other regions in both the international and domestic markets. Regional Tourism Organisations around New Zealand have increased their marketing presence, especially in the domestic market, where Wellington City has strongly positioned itself in recent years. There is also increased competition for the discretionary dollar.

Domestic Market

The domestic market has performed well in the past three years. In 1999, there were just over 740,000 domestic visitor nights in commercial accommodation, according to the Commercial Accommodation Monitor. This figure grew to nearly 840,000 in 2002. The domestic Visiting Friends and Relatives market is also very strong in Wellington; in 2002 more than 1.7 million visitor nights were spent in Wellington by visiting friends and relatives, as stated in the BRC Marketing and Social Research VFR Monitor.

Increasing Wellington's domestic marketing activity and product offering is a priority for Positively Wellington Tourism. The key will be to keep Wellington fresh and appealing by creating new reasons to visit.

For the Domestic Market, Wellington's Strengths Remain

- City excitement and nightlife
- Heritage and Nationhood
- Performing and Visual Arts
- Easy to get around/compact
- Strong VFR market
- Leisure weekend market established

Potential Lies in

- Growing the VFR market
- Events and conferences
- Family destination
- Growing the amount of weekend promotion
- Refining target marketing
- Nature close to the city
- Arts marketing
- New attractions and activities

Action Plan: Domestic Market Strategy

Positively Wellington Tourism's domestic marketing focus has moved away from the traditional target of household income in excess of $40,000. Now and in the future, it will target market segments by travel motivation. The likely mode of communication to each will reflect the travel motivation.

The Four Travel Motivations are

1. *Energising and self-expansion*: Target audience: adults without children.
   Mood: uplifting, exhilarating, invigorating, indulging, challenging.

2. *Socialising and participating*: Target audience: young singles, families and young couples.

   Mood: lively, sociable, upbeat, friendly, easy going, casual.

3. *Learning and discovery*: Target audience: singles, parents wanting to educate their children through travel. Also includes older adults.

   Mood: strong cultural or historic/heritage status.

4. *Relaxing and unwinding*: Target audience: older couples, professional people with busy lifestyles and older people.

   Mood: relaxed, down-to-earth, comfortable, safe.

The Three-pronged Domestic Approach

Positively Wellington Tourism is committed to a three pronged strategic approach to the domestic market. The aim is to deliver the most comprehensive domestic marketing campaign in New Zealand to achieve results in a range of markets.

1. *"Outside In" Marketing*: Positively Wellington campaign.
2. *"Inside Out" Marketing*: Visiting Friends and Relatives and Downtown campaigns.
3. *Events Marketing*: Leveraging key events at certain times.

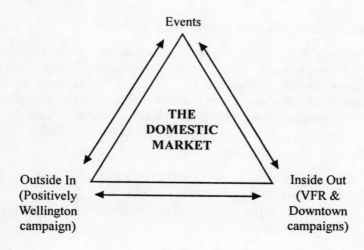

International Market

Since Positively Wellington Tourism's initial Strategy was published, Tourism New Zealand has identified the Interactive Traveller as the group that best meets New Zealand's tourism needs. It is important to understand the characteristics of the Interactive Traveller (IT) in planning international tourism marketing.

The Interactive Traveller: A Definition

The IT is a regular international traveller who consumes a wide range of tourism products and services. They seek out new experiences and demonstrate respect for natural, social and cultural environments.

The IT is likely to fall into either the 25-34 or 50-64 age bracket. They come from a range of countries, but many come from Wellington's key markets of UK, USA and Australia.

The IT chooses New Zealand primarily for the scenery and natural wonders and secondly for the culture and history. As the arts and culture capital of New Zealand, Wellington holds appeal for the IT. Positively Wellington Tourism will work to develop, in particular, the cultural tourism offering currently available for this group of international visitors.

The Australian Market

The IT from Australia is a key target of Positively Wellington Tourism's international marketing. Geographically close to New Zealand, the Australian market is considered less vulnerable to international influences such as terrorism or exchange rate fluctuations.

A General Sales Agent will continue to sell Wellington in Australia. A Public Relations agent based in Australia will continue to raise public awareness of Wellington as a great place to visit. This is in addition to a comprehensive travel trade education programme and other joint venture activity.

For the IT, Wellington's Strengths Remain

- Heritage and nationhood
- Shopping
- Easy to get around/compact size
- North-South gateway/regional gateway
- Capital City
- Performing and visual arts
- Surprise and delight factor

Potential Lies in

- Contemporary cultural tourism product
- Nature close to the city
- Learning and discovery
- More commissionable product
- Creative and Innovative City

Action Plan: International Market Strategy

Onshore activity will focus on VIN sales and training, travel network training and sales and ensuring information is available at points of entry into Wellington, such as Interisland Line Ferries and the Airport. The objective is to dramatically increase Wellington's international marketing presence onshore.

Offshore international marketing will continue to be delivered under the Centre Stage regional model.

International events are likely to influence patterns of travel in the global tourism industry. Terrorism, war and macro shifts in the world aviation market will influence Wellington's ability to grow its market. However, there are indications to suggest dramatic global events have only short term impacts on New Zealand's tourism growth. There is strong evidence to suggest that 12 to 18 months after a global event, New Zealand's inbound market tends to grow. This indicates New Zealand is perceived as a relatively safe destination.

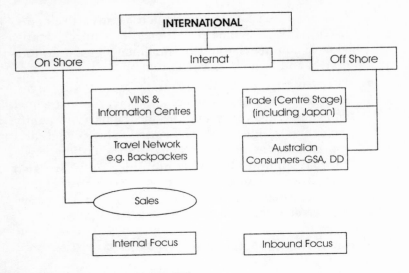

Programme of Implementation

Each of the strategic pillars has a range of sub-components. The programme of implementation outlines who are the lead and supporting agencies involved and the project timescale. In all instances, Positively Wellington Tourism is involved.

DEVELOPING A TOURISM ACTION PLAN: A CANADIAN PERSPECTIVE

A tourism action plan defines the who, what, where, when and how of making tourism happen. It provides a framework for businesses, local government and other organisations to analyse tourism resources and concerns, and to encourage development and promotion within your community.

It covers the five key components of tourism:

■ *Attractions*: natural and man-made features within and near your community that are of interest to tourists—lakes, mountains and wilderness, unique shops, historic sites, industries, fairs, conventions, competitions and tours.

- *Promotion*: marketing tools, such as advertisements, travel shows, magazine articles, brochures, maps, videos, commercial and promotional signs, auto tour guides and tourist information booths.

- *Infrastructure*: roads, airports, railways, parking areas, sewage dump stations, water and power services, boat launches, and location and distance signs. Community recreation facilities that can be used to host events and sports tournaments, such as ice arenas, curling rinks, baseball diamonds and community halls are also infrastructure elements. If access to your area is poor, and if basic services are lacking or in disrepair, tourists may go elsewhere.

Elements of a Tourism Action Plan

- An endorsement from your band council acknowledging the plan as your community's official tourism development and promotion strategy
- The plan's credentials: what it is, who developed it, under what authority and what it hopes to accomplish
- A description of the process: when and how the plan was prepared, when it will be monitored and reviewed; how it should be used and by whom, and how public input was obtained
- A definition of tourism
- The development policy for your community
- A summary of your present and potential tourism markets, assets, concerns about tourism, goals and objectives, and actions to be taken
- *Services*: hotels, motels, campgrounds, restaurants, service stations, shops and other retail businesses.
- *Hospitality*: This key element is the cement that holds the whole tourism package together. Involving everyone in your community, it determines whether tourists enjoy their stay, whether they will come back and whether they will encourage others to visit.

A committee approach to developing the plan ensures commitment from your community. It also takes advantage of the skills and experiences of community members who own businesses, work in tourism or have training in the industry.

A Band Council Resolution can formalize the committee by confirming its official name, mandate, number and selection of members and chairperson, procedures for meetings and reporting, frequency of meetings and meeting quorums.

The Committee Meeting: Agenda Tourism Development Committee Inaugural Meeting Date Place

Item

1. Selection of a chairperson
2. Selection of a secretary (if not provided by the First Nations council)
3. Review of the committee's terms of reference
4. Review of The Development of Tourism in Your Community
5. Review of background information
6. Review of the development policy, including the tourism components
7. Other business
8. Date and agenda for next meeting

During meetings, questions may arise that committee members cannot answer. Your chairperson, in consultation with the group, can designate members to collect whatever information is needed and report back to the committee by a specified deadline.

Meeting discussions and decisions should always be recorded:

- Your chairperson or an appointed member should record lists and group statements in point form on a flip chart for all to see. This can be done as the meeting proceeds to help keep the group focused on the topic.

- Your secretary should keep detailed minutes for subsequent distribution to Committee members. The minutes will form a permanent record of what takes place at each meeting.

- As each step in an activity is accomplished, your secretary should record completion.

Identify Present Tourism Markets

Before any decisions can be made, you need reliable information on the present state of tourism in your area. To establish baseline information, your committee could look at the following:

- Reasons they come. Is it for business, pleasure, for local services, to visit friends and relatives or are they just passing through?
- Services they look for and whether the services are available.
- Time of year most people visit.
- Mode of transportation.
- Length of stay.
- Amount of money they spend.
- Age, sex, education, occupation, income class and place of origin of the tourists who come to your community now.
- New trends in travel, changes in types of people travelling.

The action plan should reflect the specifics of your own community, but other communities and regional tourist associations may have information to share.

Develop Tourism Market Profiles

The chart can be used to develop profiles for each type of tourist that comes to your community at present. As previously stated, there are five types of tourists, defined according to their reason for travel:

- Business;
- Personal business;
- Vacation;
- Visiting friends and relatives; and
- Passing through.

Fill in the "present Tourism type" row for each Tourism type by answering the questions along the top of the chart. There might be potential to attract tourists from all categories, but the importance of each type of tourist to your local tourism industry will vary.

By grading present tourism markets in the column, "Present Importance," your committee can best focus on where to concentrate its efforts.

Each committee member grades each tourist type on a scale of one to 10 in importance, in terms of number, length of stay and expenditures. Ten would be the highest grade. The consensus grade is arrived at by adding up the numbers assigned to each tourist type. The tourist type with the highest grade would be ranked first; the type with the second highest grade would be ranked second, and so on.

If there are tourism operators in or near your community that are not represented on the committee, talk to them to validate your committee's findings. These tourism operators could include:

- Hotel/Motels
- Restaurants
- Parks and campgrounds
- Service stations
- Tourist information booths
- Hunting and fishing operations
- Tours
- Provincial departments of culture, tourism, parks and recreation, and transportation
- Utility departments

- Regional tourist associations
- Retail businesses
- Service clubs
- Sport and cultural events
- Tourist attractions (museums, cultural centres, etc.)

If you emphasize that the chart is still at draft stage, people will realize that their input is going to be used. This also gives you the opportunity to find out what tourism promotional activities are under way and what are planned.

At your next committee meeting, change the market profile charts according to what you have learned from these discussions.

List Tourism Assets

Tourism assets can be divided into five categories:

- Attractions
- Promotion
- Infrastructure
- Hospitality
- Services.

For example, a new elementary school is a community asset but it would also be a tourism asset if its architecture reflected First Nations influences or if it could be used for major events or conventions for tourists.

First Nations have tourism assets which are not necessarily recognized as such. These include:

- Their history and their perspectives of that history;
- Aboriginal views on nature and the environment;
- Aboriginal arts, crafts and performing arts;
- On-reserve wildlife regulatory regimes which may differ from provincial/territorial regimes;

- Reserve and nearby lands, including archaeological and historic sites, lakes, wilderness areas, wildlife habitats, vegetation and geological structures;
- Native tourism sectoral organisations which could provide valuable central services and co-ordinate the activities of First Nation communities; and
- Unique industries.

Tourism Assets

Assets	Rank
Tourism Attractions	
Provincial park nearby	1
Wilderness areas nearby with good fishing lakes	2
Annual powwow	3
Annual hockey tournament	4
Community hall	5
Community craft store/workshop	6
Tourism Promotion	
Linkages with other First Nations	1
Tourism infastructure	
Good access to primary highway	1
Full sewer and water servicing, excellent-quality water	2
Tourism Hospitality	
Some friendly merchants	1
Tourism Sevices	
New outfitter camp	2
Service station	3
Campground near reserve	1
General store	5
Tow truck service	4

Once you have listed your assets, rank them in importance. Start with tourism attractions. Have each committee member grade attractions on a scale of one to 10. Then use the grade total for each asset to determine its rank. Once you have completed ranking the attractions, go on to look at infrastructure, hospitality, service and promotion.

Recognize Tourism Concerns

Tourism concerns can include:

- *Negative assets*: Check your market profiles and list of assets for those items that may have negative aspects. Discuss how they can be improved.

- *Outright liabilities*: A noxious pulp mill on your doorstep is definitely a concern. List all such liabilities—even those that seem insurmountable—because someone else may have a partial solution. Even if no solution is found, your discussion will have helped put it into perspective for the community.

- *Undeveloped ideas*: List and discuss all ideas, no matter how off-the-wall they are. They may include great proposals that have not been acted upon. If a good suggestion is presented negatively, you then can list it as a concern, which then becomes motivation for action.

List tourism concerns the same way you listed assets.

Be explicit. For example, the statement, "Visitors just pass right through town; nobody ever stops here," is too general. It may be true, but it has to be more specific to be of use as a discussion point. Visitors may not be stopping in town because:

- There are few clean washrooms at local service stations (services).
- There are no parking spots (infrastructure).
- Tourists do not know about attractions (promotion).
- No interesting attractions are visible from the highway (attractions).
- Some merchants have not recognized the importance of being courteous to tourists (hospitality).

The more specific you are in categorizing a concern, the easier it will be to find a solution.

Rank the concerns as you did the assets. At the top of the list put obvious concerns that can be fixed easily, at little cost, and with highly visible results.

Determine Potential Tourism Markets

This exercise looks at the possibilities for increasing existing tourism and attracting an entirely new market. Using the Tourism Market Profile answer the questions along the top of the chart for the five categories of "potential new tourist types." Base your analysis on present tourism markets. For example, if existing facilities are at capacity during the summer, it might make sense to focus on winter tourists, such as snowmobilers, hockey tournament participants and spectators.

Tourism Concerns

Concerns	*Rank*
Tourism Attractions	
No major tourist attraction in community	1
No museum or cultural centre	2
Tourism Promotion	
No tourist literature	2
No welcome signs at edge of town	3
Businesses are not members of provincial and regional tourism association	6
No powwow or hockey tournament promotion outside of community	4
No community theme	1
Campers are not aware of all the goods and services available in community	5
Tourism infastructure	
Several good fishing lakes in the area without adequate access	1
No sewage dumping station for recreational vehicles in or near the community	2
Tourism Hospitality	
Some merchants and staff are unfriendly	1
Some residents are unfriendly or discourteous to visitors	2
Tourism Sevices	
Campground near reserve does not provide full service	1
No repair facilities for recreational vehicles and outboard motors in town	2
No recreational equipment rentals in town (canoes, boats, snowmobiles, etc.)	3

State Tourism Goals and Objectives

Tourism goals are clear, concise statements describing the kind of tourism wanted in your community. They must be compatible with the community's development policy and should provide direction for more specific objectives.

Tourism goals can be stated simply by inserting the phrase "to improve" in front of each of the five key components of tourism:

- To improve tourism attractions;
- To improve tourism promotion;
- To improve tourism infrastructure;
- To improve tourism hospitality; and
- To improve tourism services.

Each of these goals leads to a set of objectives which are simple, concise steps to achieving the relevant goal. They should be measurable and realistic.

How to Develop Tourism Objectives

Look at how the needs and wants on your market profile charts relate to the tourism resources of your community. Focus on one tourism goal at a time. For each goal, display your charts on present and potential market profiles, assets and concerns. Then, assign an objective to each concern. For example, tour buses may travel through your community but do not linger. How do you encourage those travellers to stay longer or to come back? The concern is that you have tourism services and attractions but no one knows about them.

For the goal, "to improve tourism promotion," your committee then develops objectives that promote businesses and services by advertising special tour services in local newspapers, provincial or territorial tourism publications or by mailing information flyers to tour companies.

The following chart provides a detailed look at the process of developing objectives.

One well-worded objective may cover more than one concern. However, avoid wording so broad or general that the objective becomes difficult to focus on or fulfil.

Once all the concerns have been matched with objectives, the objectives can be ranked to highlight the priorities. A priority list of five objectives is recommended to provide direction on what is to be achieved.

The answers to three questions help focus the relative importance of each objective.

- What present and potential markets do the objectives relate to? How important are they?
- How long will it take to accomplish the objective? (*a*) less than a year; (*b*) one to three years; or (*c*) more than three years.

What will it cost (approximately) to achieve this objective and where will the money come from?

Process for Developing Objectives

1. Display all charts completed to date.
2. Write the first goal at the top of the Tourism Goals and Objectives flip-chart.
3. Review your Tourism Market Profiles, Tourism Assets and Tourism Concerns lists related to the goal.
4. Taking the first concern on the list, ask: What can or should be done about it?
5. Write an objective related to this concern. Your first thoughts are often the best: once you have something on paper you can add, delete or amend at will. This is a time for creative thinking.
6. When everyone is satisfied with the objective, move on to the next concern and develop the next objective.

7. When all concerns relating to your first goal have been dealt with, repeat the process for the other four goals.

8. Keep a record of all proceedings.

9. After a break or at a subsequent meeting, carry out a critical review of your objectives. Make changes if you are not happy with what has been produced to this point.

The top-priority objectives should be feasible, compatible with the development policy, have highly visible results and appeal to your community members.

An example of a tourism goals and objectives is on the next page.

Develop Action Steps

Tourism action steps are specific, detailed directives on how to achieve each objective.

They must be realistic. If a proposed step leads nowhere or needs additional activities to make it work, either alter or abandon it. Otherwise, the individuals responsible for supervising its co-ordination and implementation will have an impossible task.

Tourism Action Step Work Sheet summarizes all the previous work and the elements needed to turn planning into reality. Take the information from the work sheets and lists already completed, then list action steps in the order in which you expect them to be accomplished.

If action steps are difficult to develop for a certain objective, that objective might be unrealistic and have to be changed or abandoned.

Tourism Goals and Objectives

Goal	Objectives	Rank
To improve tourism attractions	To determine what major new attraction should be pursued by the community	2
	To have the Hudson's Bay store declared a provincial historic resource	12
	To provide tourist literature	7
	To provide welcome signs on the promotion edge of town	8
To improve tourism promotion	To encourage local businesses to join the regional and provincial tourism associations	9
	To ensure that event organizers are aware of any funding available to assist in tourism promotion	5
	To establish a town theme	1
To improve tourism infastructure	To ensure that campers know about the goods and services available in town	10
	To investigate means of ensuring good access to fishing lakes	6
	To encourage businesses to use hospitality training programmes	4
To improve tourism hospitality	To establish a training programme for tourist information staff	14
	To establish a programme to ensure that all residents appreciate the need to be friendly and courteous to visitors	13
To improve tourism services	To encourage the establishment of a full-service campground	3
	To encourage the establishment of the following businesses in town: recreation vehicle service centre, 24-hour convenience store, recreation equipment rentals	11

Tourism Action Step Work Sheet

- *Goal*: To improve tourism promotion
- *Objective*: To Establish A Community Theme

- *Addressed*: No community theme
- *Justification*: What are we known for? What is our main claim to fame? Tourists will be more Rank No. 1 inclined to visit if we portray a single interesting theme.
- *Markets Implicated*: Eco-tourism, Campers, Visiting friends and relatives.
- *Time Frame*: Less than a year Expense: $500.00

Action Steps by Whom When Results

1. Develop a proposal to come up with a community theme including:
   - what criteria should be used in deciding upon it;
   - who should make the final decision;
   - how to get residents interested and involved; and
   - how the theme can be portrayed to visitors.
2. Seek assistance for the proposal from the First Nations Council and local businesses (businesses may be willing to provide prizes for the winning theme in a contest).
3. Decide on the theme.
4. Determine how best to portray the theme.
5. Institute other ways to support and promote the theme.

At this point, your committee can assign responsibility and realistic deadlines for the completion of each step. Individuals and local organisations should be encouraged to participate, but the assigned committee member is the supervisor who manages the process and reports on activities. Throughout the process, your committee is the lead player.

Involve Your Band Council and Community

Your draft tourism action plan is now ready for submission to the band council and then to the community. The draft gives both groups the opportunity to review and discuss the plan before the committee seeks input from parties outside the community.

The resulting additions or changes can be incorporated into a second draft and resubmitted to the council.

Community Input

After the band council approves the draft plan in principle, your committee can seek input from entrepreneurs, local tourism associations and government departments outside the community. The band council may have advice on when, where and how to obtain public feedback. There are various ways, including open house meetings and workshops, an open band council meeting, and presentations to local interest groups with follow-up discussion and a questionnaire. The plan can also be mailed to designated individuals with a request for feedback or can be published in the local newspaper with a request for comments or date of a public meeting. Committee members can also hold one-on-one discussions with others in the community.

Those most likely to be affected by the plan should be included at this stage. For example, if it recommends improving highway directional signs, ask the provincial highway department for comments. If key people fail to respond, have committee members visit them to explain the plan and obtain feedback.

Implement the Action Plan

The plan can be implemented only after it has received support from the band council, the community and outside private and public agencies. During this process, regular committee meetings will allow members to:

- Report on the status of action steps and develop new or alternative ones if needed;
- Undertake tasks to help accomplish objectives; and
- Deal with problems as they arise.

If you apply for advice or financial support from outside

organisations, attach a copy of the plan. It will lend substance and credibility to your application.

Outside Expertise

There are three major sources of outside expertise: consultants, published material and private tourism associations.

Use consultants only for those tasks you cannot do yourselves. Your committee is certainly in a better position to initiate the project by doing the early legwork of gathering and reviewing available information. Not only is it cheaper, but the knowledge and contacts will remain in your community.

If you do go outside your community for expertise, government tourism consultants should be able to provide sound initial advice.

When hiring consultants, be as explicit as possible in detailing the requirements. Your tourism action plan process is a good information tool for the consultant and saves briefing time.

Books are available on how to select and use consultants; how to start and run tourism businesses; and how to execute business functions, such as preparation of business plans, accounting and marketing. These books contain excellent advice at a fraction of the cost of consultants.

Private hotel and restaurant associations as well as provincial, territorial and regional tourism associations provide services to tourism businesses. Through them you can develop a network of association members who have dealt with problems similar to your own.

Monitor the Results

The procedures for monitoring the success or failure of your plan should be in place before implementation begins. Base these procedures on specific action steps and objectives.

For example, your community stages an annual powwow and you plan to promote it. Monitoring procedures need to be in place well before the event. If your objective is to attract more visitors through direct-mail promotion, newspaper and radio advertising, or a combination of these and other promotional activities, try to gauge the success of these efforts by comparing attendance figures for previous powwows with attendance figures after advertising was introduced.

Such monitoring could come in the form of sampling. Committee members or volunteers could survey a sampling of people attending the powwow with a checklist of questions, such as how they heard about the powwow, whether they have friends or relatives in the community, and where they are staying. The more people questioned, the better the sample. Encourage people to take the time to answer questions by offering such incentives as free tickets, discount coupons, pins or balloons.

Other sampling activities include questionnaires by mail and telephone interviews, but for these, you will need information on who attended and how to reach them.

Monitoring could include a status report once every six months from the committee member responsible for each objective. The report .... no more than one or two pages long .... could describe:

- The action steps that have been taken;
- The most significant results of these steps;
- The extent to which the objective has been accomplished;
- Proposed revisions, if necessary; and
- A personal comment on the validity of the objective.

After the committee reviews all the reports, they can be compiled as one document for presentation to the First Nation Council. It is also a good idea to schedule a detailed annual review to evaluate objectives. The findings of this review can be presented to the First Nation Council for consideration and endorsement.

Your community should be made aware of your committee's successes. Toot your own horn because it's a safe bet no one else will. For instance, an annual tourism night with guest speakers, films and presentations would give your chairperson an opportunity to report on achievements, to discuss what is still to be accomplished and where help is needed.

Bibliography

A.V. Seaton (ed.) (1994). *Tourism: The State of Art*, John Wiley, New York.

Airey, D. and Johnson, S. (1998). *The Profile of Tourism Studies Degree Courses in the UK: 1997-98*. London: National Liaison Group.

Aldous, T. (1972) *Battle for the Environment*, London: Fontana/ Collins.

Anderson A. Barbara, Provis Chris, and Chappel J. Shirley (2004). "The Selection and Training of Workers in the Tourism and Hospitality Industries for the Performance of Emotional Labour", *Journal of Hospitality and Tourism Management*.

Anderson, N. (1961). *Work and Leisure*, London: Routledge and Kegam Paul.

Archer, B.H. (1973). *The Impact of Domestic Tourism*, Cardiff: University of Wales Press.

Arvil, R. (1967), *Man and Environment*, Crisis and the Strategy of Choice, Penguin, Hamondsworth.

Ash, M. (1972), *Planners and Ecologists*, Town and Country Planning, Vol. 40.

Ashworth, G. (1984) *Recreation and Tourism*, London: Bell and Hayman.

Astin, A. (1990). *Assessment for Excellence*. New York: Maxwell McMillan, Inc.

Atkinson, B.W. (1981), *Precipitation in Man and Environmental Processes*, edited by K.J. Gregony and D.E. Wailing, Butterworths.

Avvill, R. (1967) *Man and Environment*, London: Penguin.

Balsdon, J.P.V.D. (1966). *Life and Leisure in Ancient Rome*, London: Bodley Head.

Bell, R. and S. Weitman (1995). "Increasing applied skills in an introductory marketing course," *Hospitality and Tourism Educator*, 7(2), pp. 11-13.

Bell, R. and S. Weitman (1995). "Increasing Applied Skills in an Introductory Marketing Course", Hospitability and Tourism Educator, 7(2), pp. 11-13.

Bharucha, M.P. (1994), Environment Compliance Litigation, *Chartered Secretary*.

Bhatt A.K. (1997). 'Human Resource Development in India' in *I.I.T.T.M. Journal of Travel and Tourism*, 1(1): 36–44.

Billings, W.D. (1964), *"Plants and Ecosystem'*, MacMillan and Co., London.

Bird, E.C.F. (1981), *Coastal Processes in Man and Environmental Processes*, edited by K.J. Gegory and D.E. Wareling, Butterworths, pp. 82-101.

Bosselman, Robert H. (1999). 'Curriculum and Instruction' in Clayton W. Barrows & Robert (editors), *Hospitality Management Education*. The Howarth Hospitality Press, New York.

Botkin, D.B. and Keller, E.A. (1982). *Environmental Studies*, C.E. Merrill Publishing Company, A Bell and Howell Company, Columbus, p. 505.

Botkin, D.B. and Keller, E.A. (1982). *Environmental Studies*, C.E. Merrill Company.

Bryan, R.B. (1981), *Soil Erosion and Conservation in Man and Environmental Processes*, edited by K.J. Gegory and D.E. Walling, Butterworths.

Bubsy, G. and P. Brunt (1997). "Tourism Sandwich Placements: An Appraisal," *Tourism Management*, Vol. 18(2).

Buhalis, D. (2003). *eTourism–Information Technology for Strategic Tourism Management*, Prentice Hall, Harlow, U.K.

Bull, A. (1991). *The Economics of Travel and Tourism*, London: Pitman.

Burkart, A.J., and S. Medlik (1974). *Tourism Past Present and Future*, Butterworth Heinemann: London.

Burton, P.E. (1988). "Building Bridges between Industry and Educations." Paper presented to Teaching Tourism into 1990, Conference University of Survey.

Butler, R.W., *"The Social Implication of Tourism Development"*, Tourism Research 2, 2(1974).

Carter, R. and Richer, P. (1999). *Marketing Tourism Destinations Online*, WTO Business Council, Madrid.

Charistou, E.S. (1999). "Hospitality Management Education in Greece", *Tourism Management*, 20:683-691.

Chidambaram R.M. (1999). Enrichment of Commerce Curriculum, University News, Vol. 137, No. 44, Nov. 1st.

Christan, E. and J. Eaton, (2000). "Management Competencies for Graduate Trainees", *Annals of Tourism Research*, Vol. 27, No. 4, pp. 1058-1061.

Chuck, Y. Gee. (1989). *The Travel Industry*, New York: Van Nostrand Reinhold.

Clapham, W.B. (1973). *'Natural Ecosystem'*, MacMillan, London.

Cloud, P.E. (1969). *'Resources and Man'*, W.H. Freeman and Company, San Francisco.

Cohen, Eric., *"Towards a Sociology of International Tourism"*, Social Research 39, 1 (1972).

Cole, M. (1971), *Plants, Animals and Environments*, Geographical Magazine, Vol. 44, pp. 230-31.

Concept C. and J. West Lake (1989). Tourism Teaching into the 1990 Tourism Management, 10(1), pp. 69-73.

Cooper, C., Scales, R. and Westlake, J. (1992). "The Anatomy of Tourism and Hospitality Educators in the UK," *Tourism Management*, 13,: 234-247.

Cosgrove, Isabel and Jackson, R. (1972). *The Geography of Recreation and Leisure*, London: Hutchinson.

Crampon, L.T. (1963). *The Development of Tourism*, Colorado: University of Colorado Press.

Cullen, Thomas P. (1988). "Filling China's Staffing Gap". The Cornell Hotel and Restaurant Administration Quarterly, 29(2), pp. 76-78.

Curtis, J.T. and McIntosh, R.P. (1950). "The Interrelations of Certain Analytical and Synthetic Phyto-sociological Characters to Study Ecology", pp. 314-34.

Dassaman, R.D. (1976), *Environmental Conservation*, Wiley, New York.

Daubernmire, R.F. (1974), *Plants and Environment*, 3rd ed., John Wiley, New York.

David Airey (1994). "Informal Tourism Employment: Vendors in Boli, Indonesia", Tourism Management 1994, 15(6) pp. 464-467.

Davis, H.D., *Potentials for Tourism of Developing Countries*, London: Finance and Development, 1968.

Det Wyler, T.R. (1971), *Man's Impact on Environment*, McGraw-Hill, New York.

Donald Hawkins and John D. Hunt, "Travel and Tourism Professional Education" *International Journal of Management and Tourism*, pp. 349-362.

Donald, E. Hawking (Eds.), *Tourism Planning and Development Issues*, Washington: George Washington University, 1980.

Dumazedier, J. (1967). *Towards a Society of Leisure*, New York: Free Press.

Eaton, J., and Christau, E. (1997). "Hospitality Management Competencies for Graduate Trainees: Employers' View", *Journal of European Business Education*, 7(1), pp. 60-68.

Edgell, D. (1990). "International Tourism Policy," New Work: Van Nostrand.

Edmunds, *Environmental Administration*, New York: McGraw-Hill, 1973.

Edward, J. Mayo (1981). *The Psychology of Leisure Travel*, Boston: CBI Publishing Company.

Evangelos Christou (1999). "Hospitality Management Education in Greece–An Exploratory Study", Tourism Management, 20 (1999), pp. 683-691.

Fitzgerald, M.J. and Cullen, T.P. (1991). "Learning through a "Read World" experience, The Cornell Hotel and Restaurant Adminis-tration Quarterly, August, pp. 85-88.

Foster, D. (1985). *Travel and Tourism Management*, London: Macmillan.

Furley, P.A. and Newey, W.W. (1983), *Man and the Biosphere*, Butterworths, London.

Gamble, P.R. (1992). "The Educational Challenge for Hospitality and Tourism", *Tourism Management*, March: 6-10.

Gearing Charles, E. (1976). *Planning for Tourism Development*, New York: Praeger Publishers.

George E. (2004). Medical Tourism: Tamil Nadu's Top Agenda. By Laxmi Subramanian. *Express Travel and Tourism*. Vol. 17, No. 10, October.

Ghodsee Kristen (2003). Executive Summary of Research Present-ation: Women Employment, and Tourism in Post Totalitarian Bulgaria.

Go, E.M., (1994). Emerging Issues in Tourism Education, in W. Theobald (ed.) Global. Tourism–The Next Decade, Oxford, Butterworth–Heinemann.

Hammarskjold, K. (1972). *"Economics of Air Transport and Tourism"*, Montreal: I.C.A.O.

Hawkins and D. Hunt (1988). "Travel and tourism professional education Hospitality and tourism educator, Spring.

Hawkins, D.E. and Hunt, T.D., (1980). Travel and Tourism Professional Education, Hospitality and Tourism Educator (1), pp. 7–13.

Haywood, K.M. and K. Maki (1992). "A Conceptual Model of the Education/Employment Interface for Tourism Industry", pp. 237-248 in Ritchie. JRB and Hawkins, D(eds), World Travel and Tourism Review CAB, Oxford.

Heath, E. (1992). *Marketing Tourism Destinations*, New York: Wiley.

Hegarts Joseph A. (1990). "Challenges and Tourism Education Programmes in Developing Countries", Hospitality and Tourism Educator 2(3): pp. 12–15.

Higgins, R.B., (1996). The Global Structure of the Nature tourism industry: Ecotourist, tour operators, and local businesses, *Journal of Travel Research*, 32(2), pp. 11–18.

Hodyson, A. (1987). *The Travel and Tourism Industry*, Oxford: Pergamon.

Hollander, S. (1968). *Passenger Transportation*, Michigan: Michigan State University.

Holliman, J. (1974), *Consumer's Guide to the Protection of the Environment*, Ballanine, London.

Hospitality Training Foundations, Labor Market Review (2000). "The Scene in the UK".

Hunt, J.D., and Higgins, B. (1981). "Proposed Undergraduate Programs in Travel and Tourism". The George Washington University.

Hunziker, W. (1951). *Social Tourism: Its Nature and Problems*, Geneva: Aliance International de Turisme.

Hurdman, L.E. (1980). *Tourism: A Shrinking World*, New York: Wiley.

Imandar D.B. (2003). Karnataka Tourism Taps Healthcare Sector, *Express Travel and Tourism,* Vol. 6, No. 18, July 16-31.

Inkpen, G. (1998). *Information Technology for Travel and Tourism*, Addison Wesley Longman, Essex UK.

Jafari, J. (1990). Research and Scholarship: The Basis of Tourism Education. The *Journal of Tourism Studies*, Vol. 1, No. 1.

Jenkins, C.L., (1980). Education for Tourism Policy Makers in Developing Countries, *International Journal of Tourism Management,* Dec., 1980, pp. 238-42.

Joseph, D. Firdgen, *Dimensions of Tourism*, East Lansing, Michigan: American Hotel and Motel Association, 1991.

Joshi Anuradha, (1999). *Value Development among Youths*, University News, Vol. 37, No. 43, Oct. 25th.

Kerry Godrey and Jackie Clarke (2000). *The Tourism Development Handbook*, London: Cassell.

Khan, Olsen Var (ed.) (1993). *VNR's Encyclopedia of Hospitality and Tourism*, New York.

Ladki, M. (1993). "Hospitality Education: the Identity Struggle", *International Journal of Hospitality Management*, Vol. 12 No., 3, pp. 243-251.

Law, C. (1993). *Urban Tourism: Attracting Visitors to Large Cities*, London: Mansell.

Laws, E. (Ed.) (1997). *The ATTT Tourism Education Handbook*, Tourism Society, London.

Laws, E.C. (1995). *Tourist Destination Management: Issues, Analysis and Policies*, London: Routledge.

Lawson, Maclom (1975). *Teaching Tourism Education and Training in Western Europe: A Comparative Study*, London: Tourism International Press.

Lee, N. and Wood, C. (1972), *Planning and Pollution*, The Planner, Vol. 58, pp. 153-58.

Leslie D., MewAleenan, M. (1990). The Indo Trial Placement Experience in the U.K. Students, *Journal of Industry and Higher Education*, 4(1), pp. 15-22.

Lickorish, L.J. (1953). *Tourism and International Balance of Payments*, Geneva: International Institute of Scientific Travel Research.

Lieper, N. (1995). *Tourism Management*, RIMT Publishing, Melbourne.

Luke, D., and A. Ingold, (1990). "Planning for Industry: A Study in Curriculum Design." *International Journal of Contemporary Hospitality Management*, 2(2), pp. 20-23.

Marsh, G.P. (1984), *Man and Nature* (Physical Geography as modified by Human Action), Charles Scribner, New York.

Mash, R. (1989). *The Rights of Nature*, University of Wisconsin Press, Madison.

Matsieson, A. (1982). *Tourism: Economic, Physical and Social Impacts*, London, Longman.

Medlik, S. (1972). *Economic Importance of Tourism*, Surrey: University of Surrey.

Middleton V.T.C., Ladkin, A. (1996). *The Profiles of Tourism Studies Degree Courses in UK: 1995/6*, National Liaison Group, London.

Mill, R.C. and Morrison, A.M. (1986). "The Tourism System." Englewood.

Milman Ady, Peter Ricci (2004). "Predicting Job Retention of Hourly Employees in the Lodging Industry", *Journal of Hospitality and Tourism Research*, Vol. No. 21(2), pp. 28-40.

Murphy, P.E. (1985). *Tourism: A Community Approach, Methuen*, New York.

Nelson, I.G. and Byrne, A.B. (1986), *Man as an Instrument of Landscape Change*, Alberta Geog. Rev., Vol. 58, pp. 226-38.

Nicholson, M. (1977). The Environmental Revolution, London: Penguin.

O'Connor, P. (1999). Electronic Information Distribution in Tourism and Hospitality, CABI Publishing, U.K.

Odum, H.T. (1971), *Environment, Power and Society*, Wiley Interscience, New York.

Okeivi, F.D. Fruley and Postel, R.T. (1994). "Food and Beverage Management Education, 6(4), pp. 37-40.

Parker, S. (1971). *The Future of Work and Leisure*, London: Mac Gibbon and Kee.

Peaker, A. (1973). *"Holiday Spending by the British at Home and Abroad"*, National Westminster Bank Quarterly Review, August.

Pearce, Sales, J. (1959). *Travel and Tourism Encyclopedia*, London: Blandford.

Philips E.A. (1959). "Methods of Vegetation Study", A Holt Dryden Book. Henry Hott and Co. Inc., p. 107.

Raymond, F. (1978). *Ecological Principles for Economic Development*, London: John Wiley.

Rebecca Shephered and Chris Cooper (1995). "Innovations in Tourism Educating and Training", Tourism Recreational Research, Vol. 20 (2), 1995, pp. 14-42.

Richards, G. (1972). *Tourism and the Economy*, Surrey: University of Surrey.

Ritche, J.R.B. (1988). "Alternative approaches to teaching tourism", paper presented at Teaching Tourism in to the work-based 1990s Conference, University of Survey.

Robinson, H.A. (1976). *Geography of Tourism*, London: MacDonald and Evans.

Ross, G.F. (1994). *The Psychology of Tourism*, Melbourne: Hospitality Press.

Ryan, C. (1991). *Recreational Tourism: A Social Science Perspective*, London: Routledge.

Sanes, C. (1996). Employees Impact on Service Delivery, Management Development Review, 9(2), pp. 15-20.

Seldin, P. (1988). Evaluating College Teaching. College Teaching and Learning: Preparing for New Commitments. *In New Directions for Teaching and Learning*. Young, R.E. and Eble, K.E. (Eds.) San Francisco: Jossey-Bass Publishers.

Sharpley Richard, Foster Gill, (2003). "The Implications of Hotel Employee Attitudes for the Development of Quality Tourism: The Case of Cyprus", *Tourism Management*, Vol. 24, pp. 687-697.

Sheldon, P. (1997). *Tourism Information Technology*, CA International, Wallingford, UK and New York, USA.

Shen B., and Z. Liu (1999). *Principles of Tourism Studies*, Xue Lin Publishing House, Shanghai.

Simmons, I.G. (1974), *The Ecology and Natural Resources*, Edward Arnold, London.

Smith, K.S. and Simpson, R.D. (1995). Validating Teaching Competencies for Faculty Members in Higher Education: A National Study Using the Delphi Method. *Innovative Higher Education, 19.*

Sophee Elias (1992). The future of Tourism and Hospitality Management Courses. Tourism Management, March 1992, pp. 137-140.

Sorensen (1973). "Environment Impact Assessment", Wild Life Institute of India, D.Dun. (U.P.); Selected readings—A Review General, Version 2000.

Stuart A. Schulman and Joseph A. Greenburg "Two Year College Tourism Education: A Study of Institution Satisfaction and Linkage, *International Journal of Management and Tourism...* pp. 101-108.

Tas, R. (1988). "Teaching Future Managers", *The Cornell Hotel and Restaurant Administration Quarterly*, 29(2), pp. 41-43.

Tribe J. (1997). "The Indiscipline of Tourism," *Annals of Tourism Research*, Vol. 24(3), pp. 638-657.

Turgut Var and Dr. Sang-Mu Kim, "Tourism Education in Korea", International Journal of Management and Tourism.

Umbreit, W.T. (1992). "In search for Hospitality Curriculum Relevance for the 1990's," *Hospitality and Tourism Educator*, 15(1), pp. 71-74.

Verma Shashi (2004). Towards an Effective University—*Industry Interaction: A Tripod Approach*, University New, Vol. 42, No. 32, August.

Vose, Richard (1995). Tourism: The Human Perspective, Hodder and Stoughtan Educational, London.

Wahab S., Hammam, A. and Jafari, J. (1998). "Tourism Education and Training", *Annals of Tourism Research*, Vol. 25(2), pp. 527-528.

Walle, A.H., (1997). A Conference Report, "Graduate Education and Research" Annals of Tourism Research, Vol. 24 (3), pp. 754-756.

Whittaker, R.H. (1975), *Communities and Ecosystem*, 2nd ed. MacMillan, New York.

Wong Simon, Pang Loretta, (2003). "Motivators to creativity in the hotel industry-perspectives of Managers and Supervisors", *Journal of Tourism Management*, Vol. 24, pp. 551-559.

Woods, H., Robert, Viehland Douglas, "Women in Hotel Management", *Cornel Hotel and Restaurant Administration Quartely*, US.

World Travel and Tourism Council (2004). Travel and Tourism in India. *The Economic Impact and Potential*, London.

Index